THE VICEROYS

AND GOVERNORS-GENERAL
OF INDIA 1757-1947

a

THE VICEROYS

AND GOVERNORS-GENERAL

OF INDIA 1757-1947

By VISCOUNT MERSEY
(Clive Bigham Mersey)

Biography Index Reprint Series

Originally published by
JOHN MURRAY
London

 BOOKS FOR LIBRARIES PRESS
FREEPORT, NEW YORK

First Published 1949

Reprinted 1971 by arrangement with
John Murray, Publishers, Ltd.

INTERNATIONAL STANDARD BOOK NUMBER:
0-8369-8088-3

LIBRARY OF CONGRESS CATALOG CARD NUMBER:
70-160925

PRINTED IN THE UNITED STATES OF AMERICA

PREFACE

THESE short sketches of the lives of the thirty-three English, Scots and Irish men who during a period of nearly two centuries have ruled India are a modest attempt to assemble their records in a limited compass as much with reference to their early and later careers as to the time they spent in India. The writer has not tried to present a consecutive history of the Indian Empire, of which he has no special knowledge, though he has travelled in it and its adjoining countries, has served as a member of a Round Table Conference, and has known personally ten of its Viceroys, so that he has some slight realisation of the labours, difficulties and limitations with which they were always beset. Of the more recent Viceroys, of whom four are still living, the accounts given are mainly factual: for sufficient time has not yet elapsed, nor is sufficient knowledge available, to assess a fair appreciation of their work.

He wishes to thank the Duke of Portland, Lords Linlithgow, Reading, Willingdon, Elgin, Minto, Halifax, Wavell, Mountbatten, St Davids, Chelmsford, Hardinge of Penshurst, the former India Office, the National Portrait Gallery, and All Souls College, Oxford, for their kindness in lending portraits or supplying information which have been of much assistance to him.

CONTENTS

CONTENTS

LIST OF ILLUSTRATIONS

ix

LIST OF ILLUSTRATIONS

LIST OF ILLUSTRATIONS

* By courtesy of the High Commissioner for India.

Cras hodierna leges, post annos Caesaris acta;
Parva decet propius cernere, magna procul.

INTRODUCTION

THE peninsula of Hindustan, containing one-quarter of the world's population, of various races, faiths and tongues, though fenced by mountains and seas, has often been invaded in the last three thousand years, usually by Asiatics. Alexander of Macedon held a small portion of it for a short time in the fourth century B.C.; and after him Scythians, Arabs, Mongols, Afghans and Persians in turn subdued parts of the North. In A.D. 1526, Baber, a petty Mohammedan prince from Central Asia, but a descendant of Genghis and Tamerlane, entered the Punjab from Afghanistan; and during the next two centuries the so-called Mogul Empire under his successors Akbar, Jehangir, Shah Jehan and Aurungzib gradually extended its sway until eventually it stretched from the Himalayas almost to Cape Comorin; for there was no united Indian people to oppose it.

But the Mogul Government, though splendid and at first powerful, became cumbrous and corrupt: and as its central control weakened, distant lieutenants, Vizirs, Nawabs, Rajahs and Amirs, set up independent kingdoms for themselves though still acknowledging the suzerainty of the Emperor at Delhi.

In the meanwhile European traders from the Western seas—Portuguese, Dutch, French and English—had established small settlements along the Indian coasts which developed on a considerable scale. For their security they found it necessary to set up stations, factories and warehouses which they· protected by defences; and by grants, leases and loans they gradually acquired lands and trading facilities from the neighbouring native princes. The chief of these were: in the South, the Nizam of Hyderabad, a Moslem prince ruling Hindus, his deputy

A   1

the Nawab of the Carnatic and the Rajah of Mysore; in the North, the Vizir of Oudh and the Nawab of Bengal, a number of Sikh and Punjab Amirs, and the Maharajah of Kashmir, a Hindu ruling Moslems; in the West and Centre the Peshwa of Poona and the great Mahratta chiefs, Holkar and Scindia, besides many smaller potentates; and in the East, the Kings of Burma and Ava.

The English had three main stations or Presidencies as they came to be called: at Madras (Fort St George), Calcutta (Fort William) and Bombay, each ruled by a council of merchants and controlled from home by the wealthy East India Company, which had obtained its first charter from Queen Elizabeth in the year 1600. The English had more effective sea power and communication, shrewder ideas of business, and were perhaps more concerned with trade than the other Western nations whom they gradually surpassed or dispossessed. They acquired a reputation for useful and honest dealing and were soon allowed to enlist native troops or Sepoys who were officered by Englishmen. Calcutta, situated on the Hugli, an estuary of the Ganges, became their headquarters, and it grew rapidly in riches. The East India Company also controlled the China trade, which later became largely concerned with opium.

The English were fortunate in having from the first active and courageous men to guide them. Of these, Robert Clive and Warren Hastings, two civilian servants of the Company at Madras, led the way; and after them came a succession of Governors-General and Viceroys, supported by an Army and a Civil Service, who first conquered, then pacified, ruled and educated, and have now after two hundred years transferred again to the inhabitants of India the empire of their own land.

The Mogul dynasty flourished for a slightly longer period than the British Raj; but the extent of its dominions and the progress and prosperity of its subjects had been far less, though the taxation it had imposed was heavier. Indeed, the record of British administration can safely compare in strength and security with anything similar since the days of Augustus and Trajan.

In 1774, the year in which George Washington was elected the first President of the United States of America, Warren Hastings was appointed Governor-General of Bengal, and British losses in one Continent were off-set by her gains in another.

In the early days of British rule there were difficulties and wars in different Indian states, with the Mahrattas, the Pindaris and the Sikhs: and in 1857 a dangerous mutiny among the Sepoy troops nearly overwhelmed Northern India. After its suppression the duties and powers of the East India Company were taken over by the British Crown; and for the last ninety years India has been governed by Viceroys, assisted by a small Executive and later by a larger Legislative Council, but in effect, and until quite recently, autocrats. British India, consisting of the Presidencies and Provinces, was under Calcutta, while the so-called Princely States were ruled by their hereditary chiefs, who usually had a British Resident at their Courts. In 1912 the capital was moved from Calcutta to New Delhi as being more central.

The small original garrisons of Sepoys were first supplemented by King's Troops in 1754; a numerical proportion varying from two to one to three to one being kept between the two forces. Seventy-seven per cent. of the Indian Army came from the Punjab or the North-West Provinces.

Under Clive and Hastings regular administrative services were set up; and in course of time the English code of law was imposed in major matters and English became the official language.

The Governor-General had at first two masters—the Company, which wanted dividends, and the President of the Board of Control in London, who was supposed to direct policy. After the transfer of power to the Crown the commercial side disappeared; and a Secretary of State at Whitehall then replaced the Board of Control. But in the last resort it was the Viceroy who took the effective decision, being both Head of the State and Prime Minister, positions which made him probably the most powerful, one of the hardest-worked and the most responsible ruler in the world.

The English never interfered with native religions though they modified some of their more barbaric practices, nor did they attempt their conversion to Christianity. The native population, under fixed and known laws, were as a rule allowed freedom of speech, freedom from arbitrary arrest, which they had never had before, and later on freedom of the press; and they were gradually given an increasing measure of self-government by elected bodies.

Early in the present century ideas of independence had germinated in India. A new generation had arisen since the Mutiny, the memories of which were being forgotten; free education had widened the views of many natives, some of whom had acquired in Europe a democratic and legalistic outlook inspired both by moral and material hopes. The Civil Service was being largely Indianised; there was an able and active Indian Bar and a rich and expanding Indian commercial community. In England a sympathetic Liberal Government was strongly established; and the system of elected councils with political debates and press campaigns had led to the birth of an independent Congress which was stimulated by a wave of self-determination in Europe and Asia and by the example of several revolutionary movements in other countries. England offered the Morley–Minto reforms in 1909 and the Montagu–Chelmsford reforms some ten years later; while the First World War had shown that she was not invulnerable and possibly not invincible. Perhaps British mentality was allergic to the educated Oriental, perhaps the great bureaucratic machine, long the cynosure of all Civil Services, was beginning to creak; but things were out of gear. There was plenty of sympathy from abroad; and continuous powerful racial and religious proselytism in India itself. The second and even more exhausting World War followed; and the Indians would have been more than human had they not profited by such a heaven-sent opportunity.

England played a friendly and honest though restrained part, not perhaps always appreciated, towards the Independence movement. In 1935 Ministerial self-government was accorded to eleven provinces of British India; and in 1942 a Cabinet Mission under Sir Stafford Cripps offered India the long-promised Dominion status, which for different reasons was refused both by Hindus and Moslems. At last, in 1947, complete independence was accorded; and three new states were set up: Pakistan, mainly Moslem, in the North; India (Hindustan), mainly Hindu, in the rest of the peninsula; and Burma in the East. The two first of these remain within the Commonwealth.* Some of the Princely States acceded to the new republics. By this voluntary resignation of power, for which history has no precedent, a population of 200 million Hindus, 100 million Moslems and Sikhs, 50 million Depressed Classes and 80 million inhabitants of the 600 Princely States, speaking a dozen different languages, were handed over to their own complete control. The world awaits the result.

* See page 168.

N. Dance pinx.

ROBERT CLIVE

LORD CLIVE

1

LORD CLIVE

Governor of Bengal 1758-1760 and 1765-1767

ROBERT CLIVE, the eldest son of Richard Clive, an impoverished squire of an old family in Shropshire, was born at Styche in that county on Michaelmas Day, 1725. His mother was Rebecca Gaskell of Manchester, whose sister married a son of the 12th Lord Sempill.

He was educated at four private schools, where he was much less noted for book learning or scholastic diligence than for outdoor adventure, pugnacity and leadership. At the age of eighteen he was nominated to a writer's post in the East India Company's establishment at Madras; and in the course of his long sea voyage to that place he spent nine months in Brazil, where he learned a little Portuguese and contracted some debts. In Madras he had no friends, and he found the indoor life there so tedious and depressing that he fell into a melancholy—an illness to which he always remained subject—and even tried to shoot himself; but his pistol failed him, an escape which convinced him that he had been saved for some definite future; for he had a strong streak of religion.

At this time the commercial settlements of the different European Powers in India—French, English, Dutch and Portuguese—were in constant trade rivalry, intriguing with the neighbouring native princes and offering or receiving money or military aid. The employees of the English Company also did business on their own behalf; and there was much corruption and giving and taking of bribes. In 1744, the year of Clive's arrival, war had just broken out in Europe between France and England; and this was soon reflected in their Indian settlements. An attack was made on Madras by the French Admiral Labourdonnais, who captured the town with its inhabitants; and Clive and his fellow-clerks became prisoners on parole. But in Clive's view the French did not observe the terms of capitulation; so he seized the chance of escaping in native dress with a friend, and arrived at the small neighbouring English fort of St David. His active instincts then quickly became warlike; he obtained an ensign's commission, and in the ensuing siege of Pondicherry distinguished himself by exceptional bravery.

The peace of Aix-la-Chapelle sent him back to his desk; but he had now found where his tastes and his abilities lay. Without any military training or connection he had a soldier's spirit, an active mind and body, and an indomitable will to succeed. In the counting-house he had learnt how to deal with the natives in business, though he spoke little Hindustani; he now learned how to lead or fight them in the field. Among his English comrades in the settlement his disregard of danger was proverbial. In a duel about cards, when he had fired his own shot in the air, his opponent came up to him, put his pistol to Clive's head and said: "Ask for your life or I will fire." "Fire and be damned," said Clive; "I said you had cheated, and I will never apologise." This part of his career reads like a novel of Charles Lever's or Fenimore Cooper's; but it seems that he was seldom the aggressor.

His next exploit was leading a storming party against the fort of Devikota in an attempt by the English to reinstate a Mahratta prince. Clive, now a lieutenant, was left alone with only thirty men, but he nevertheless continued to advance with his usual audacity until supports arrived and the fort was taken. His commander, Major Stringer Lawrence, now got him the post of commissary for provisioning the troops and convoying supplies. Lawrence, an excellent soldier himself, called Clive "A man of un-daunted resolution, of a cool temper and of a presence of mind that never left him." The Sepoys adored him.

Clive soon fell ill of another nervous fever and was sent up the coast to Bengal to recuperate; and on his return to Fort St David he was promoted captain. The English authorities there were endeavouring to relieve Trichinopoly, where one of their native allies was besieged by a rival, Chanda Sahib, who was supported by Dupleix, the French Governor of Pondicherry. The English were not doing well; so to create a diversion Clive suggested an attack on Arcot, the capital of the Carnatic, as the eastern sea-coast of the Deccan was then called. His advice was accepted; and he was sent in command of the raid with 200 English, 200 Sepoys and 3 guns. By a *coup de main* he occupied the fort and then followed up and defeated the retreating garrison. This move forced Chanda Sahib to transfer a large portion of his forces from Trichinopoly to Arcot, where he was twice beaten by Clive, who later withstood a siege of fifty days with far less troops, guns and supplies than his enemy; and eventually both the French and native commanders capitulated. By this success and by Clive's personal bravery British prestige in the South of India was raised to a great height; he had been constantly in the front line, inspiring his men and running every risk. But the effects of the campaign again told upon his health; and in 1753 he was given sick leave to return to England. Before sailing he married Margaret Maskelyne, a sister of the comrade with whom he had escaped from Madras and daughter of a Wiltshire gentle-man. He was just twenty-seven years old.

Clive was received with acclamation by the directors of the East India Company in London. Traders them-selves, they were mainly concerned with their own profits, and they welcomed the advent of a young servant who evidently had military and diplomatic as well as commercial qualities. They voted him a diamond-studded sword and hailed him as a future general.

Clive had brought home a good deal of prize money, much of which he devoted to relieving his family's financial difficulties, buying back their old estate and providing for his sisters. He spent freely, and fought an expensive election in Cornwall, though he was unseated on petition. Restored in health and short of funds—he had only £3000 left—he was soon ready to return to India. The directors now appointed him Lieutenant-Governor of Fort St David with the reversion of the governorship of Madras; and he was made a lieutenant-colonel. He arrived in Bombay in the spring of 1756, and after taking part in an expedition against a local brigand he went on to Fort St David, arriving there on the day before the capture of Calcutta by Surajah Dowlah, the young Nawab of Bengal, and the subsequent tragedy of the Black Hole.

On receipt of this news in Madras, Clive was chosen to take a relieving force up to Bengal with a mixed contingent of over 2000 troops. He did not reach the Hugli until December, but then with little difficulty retook Calcutta. The Nawab, a youth of ungovernable temper, advanced against him with 40,000 foot and horse and some French artillery. Clive with a force of one-twentieth of their number easily drove them away; and a peace was patched up. But the Nawab continued to intrigue with the French and again threatened Calcutta from the neighbourhood of Plassey. A long and devious negotiation followed, not apparently very creditable to Clive, who made use of two dissimilar draft treaties, one on white and the other on red paper, and so deceived his Hindu go-between, Omichand, who had pledged his name to Clive's rival candidate Mir Jafar. Surajah Dowlah's army had now risen to 50,000 men, while Clive had only 1000 British troops and 2000 Sepoys. He lay in a grove near the river Hugli and at first determined on the advice of his officers not to attack; but during the night he changed his mind, and having succeeded in putting the French guns out of action, with the support of Mir Jafar's cavalry he utterly routed the whole of the Nawab's army on 23rd June 1757. Surajah Dowlah was taken prisoner and put to death; Mir Jafar was installed as Nawab in his place; and large sums of money were paid as compensation to the East India Company, Clive himself receiving a quarter of a million sterling as a personal gift.

From this victory, a scrimmage, but one of the decisive battles of the world, British dominion in India is usually held to date, for it was as much a blow to the French as to the Mogul Emperor and his subordinate princes. Clive's genuine belief was that only one European nation could be in control in India; and his policy was to eliminate the others as opportunity offered. He was now appointed Governor of the Company's possessions in Bengal, and there he remained for two years. He did not neglect British interests in the South, though he clearly informed the Board at home that Calcutta should be the centre of their power; nor did he hesitate to tell his directors how they should manage their business. The elder Pitt agreed with his forward policy and had as great an admiration for Clive as Clive had for him, though Clive always said that peace was the most valuable of all blessings.

In 1760 he again returned to England. He was received by the young King, George III, to whom he gave a large diamond; was described by Pitt as a "heaven-born General," and was honoured by many public ovations. But for twelve months he was again laid up, and it was not until his recovery that his successes were officially recognised. He was then created an Irish peer, made a Knight of the Bath, and elected M.P. for Shrewsbury, a seat he kept for the rest of his life; but his request for a British peerage was not granted. In Parliament he supported George Grenville's administration, though he took little part in domestic politics. Nottingham and Henry Fox were his friends, as was his powerful country neighbour, Lord Powis.

But during Clive's absence in England misgovernment and corruption had increased in Bengal. Mir Jafar had been deposed; some Sepoy regiments had mutinied, and another massacre of Europeans had taken place at Patna. The directors at the India House became nervous; and in 1764 Clive was asked to return to India as Governor of Bengal. He arrived there in May 1765. In the words of Sir William Hunter: "The beginning of our Indian rule dates from this second governorship of Clive's, as our military supremacy had dated from his victory at Plassey.

"Clive landed, advanced rapidly from Calcutta to Allahabad, and there settled in person the fate of nearly half India. . . . Two landmarks stand out in his policy. First, he sought the substance, though not the name, of territorial power, under the fiction of a grant from the Mogul Emperor; second, he desired to purify the Company's service by prohibiting illicit gains and by guaranteeing a reasonable pay from honest sources." Of both these policies he laid the foundation, acquiring the rich provinces of Bengal, Behar and Orissa, with 25 million subjects; confirming the British position in the Deccan and Madras, where a so-called rent was paid both to the Emperor and to the Nizam of Hyderabad, and starting the model of the Indian Civil Service.

When Clive quitted India for the last time in 1767 his name and reputation there stood high; and the men he left behind him, Vansittart and Warren Hastings, had been well chosen. But on arriving in England he found that his position there had greatly changed. He brought home no more crores of rupees, for he had been setting the military and civil employees an example of obeying his own rules, and had indeed devoted a large part of his private fortune to a fund for those who had been disabled by their

Indian service. At the India House a hostile faction, led by a Mr Sullivan, constantly attacked him not only for misgovernment but for peculation, charges to which Clive replied in the House of Commons in a speech which Lord Chatham described as the finest he had ever heard. A Committee of Enquiry was set up at which Clive defended himself with vigour and success, making the well-known remark: "By God, Mr Chairman, I stand in this place astonished at my own moderation." From this ordeal he emerged victorious, for though the Committee found him guilty of abusing his powers, they carried a resolution that "he had rendered great and meritorious service to the State."

But Clive was deeply distressed by his treatment, which had begun to prey on his mind and his health. In December 1767 he was unable to write with his own hand and considered wintering abroad. He was suffering from gallstones, and to relieve the pain he now had recourse to opium. He lived more in the country than in London, for he had bought an estate at Walcot and a good deal of land round Bishop's Castle, where he controlled the borough—he was known as a great "boroughmonger"—and he was the principal Government authority on Indian matters. He had also been made Lord-Lieutenant of both Shropshire and Montgomery. But his life's occupation was gone; he felt ill-used and disappointed; and the melancholy from which he had often suffered now affected his mind. In November 1774, soon after his forty-ninth birthday, he cut his throat in his sitting-room in Berkeley Square. He was buried in Westminster Abbey.

He left several children; and ten years after his death his eldest son married the sister and heiress of the last Earl of Powis of the Herbert family, a title that was revived in his favour in 1804. The present Earl of Powis is his direct male descendant.

Clive passed little more than twelve years of his life in

India; in that short space of time all his work there was done. The fortune he had brought home, though large, was nothing to what it might have been had he taken advantage of all his opportunities. He preferred to leave his country a greater legacy in the victories he had gained and the example he had set in the government of a new empire. A religious man, of rough manners and appearance, affectionate to his family and full of ambition for himself, he was also a genuine patriot with high ideals and the strength of will to implement them. Of remarkable courage in war and ability in diplomacy, he was able to see ahead and to indicate the lines on which his beliefs should be developed. Though he never actually held the office of Governor-General of India, he in fact exercised much of its powers, and he can rightly be reckoned as the first of the long and distinguished line of those who have filled that imperial post.

Sir T. Lawrence pinx.

WARREN HASTINGS

2

WARREN HASTINGS

Governor of Bengal 1772-1774
Governor-General 1774-1785

WARREN HASTINGS was born at Churchill in Oxfordshire on 18th December 1732. His father and grandfather were both named Peniston Hastings, the latter being Rector of Daylesford, part of an estate which had formerly belonged to their family, which was said to be a distant branch of the noble race of the Earls of Huntingdon. They had latterly fallen into reduced circumstances; and as Warren Hastings lost his father early, he was educated at the expense of an uncle who had a place in the Customs. His mother, Hester Warren, was the daughter of a farmer.

At the age of fifteen Hastings became the first King's Scholar of his year at Westminster, where the poet Cowper, Elijah Impey and the future Lord Shelburne were his schoolfellows. There he shewed great merit and in 1750 he was nominated to a clerkship in the East India Company's service.

After two years' work in Calcutta he was sent inland to Kasim Bazar, the trading quarter of Murshidabad, which was then the centre of the native government; and two years later he was made a member of the local council.

In 1756 the Nawab of Bengal, Surajah Dowlah, seized Calcutta; and Warren Hastings was imprisoned, but was soon released. He joined some of his Calcutta colleagues who had taken refuge in a fort at Falta, and was able by his influence with the natives to procure them provisions. His conduct here was of such value that after the reconquest of Calcutta he was sent by Clive as Resident to Murshidabad. He had just married the widow of a Captain Buchanan, a daughter of Colonel C. F. Scott. By her he had two children, who, with their mother, died a few years later.

In 1761 Hastings was appointed to the Council at Calcutta, where John Holwell had become Governor on Clive's leaving for England. He was given the difficult task of arranging terms between the new Nawab and the English factory at Patna on the question of trading dues. In this he did not succeed, but he drafted some proposals for regulating the trade which the Nawab accepted and which commended themselves to Vansittart, who was now acting as Governor; but they did not secure the Council's approval; and in consequence Hastings was abused by both parties. Patna was then attacked by the English, and the chief of the trading station and many of the employees were killed by the Nawab's orders, who was, however, soon afterwards defeated and banished. Throughout this affair Hastings shewed himself capable of diplomacy and courage.

At the end of 1764 he returned to London on leave, and there he remained for four years in poor circumstances, for he had brought home little money. He managed, however, to buy a small annuity for the widow of the uncle who had educated him. He kept closely in touch with Indian affairs and with the India House, and gave evidence before a Committee of the House of Commons which much impressed the directors. He also interested himself in plans for the future education of civil employees of the Company, and even tried to have a Persian scholarship founded at Oxford. During this time he was much concerned in literature and literary society, meeting Dr Johnson and some of his friends; but his real wish was to get back to India, to improve his position and his income.

When, early in 1769, he was appointed as second in council at Madras, he had to borrow his passage money.

On board the ship by which he sailed there was a German Baron von Imhoff, a portrait painter under the protection of Queen Charlotte, who was seeking employment in India. During the journey Hastings fell ill and was nursed by the Baroness, with whom he fell in love. From Madras Imhoff went on to Calcutta, leaving his wife behind; and when a year later Hastings was appointed Governor of Bengal she followed him there.

At this time, although the immediate neighbourhood of Calcutta was at peace, the finances were in a state of confusion, for extortion and corruption were again spreading. Anxious to remedy this, Hastings set up a system by which native officials were to collect the revenue under English supervisors. This caused much bad blood among those who were dispossessed, and also brought in an insufficient revenue to the Company.

In England Lord North's Regulating Act had recently been passed by which a Governor-General of Bengal with a small Council was to administer the British possessions in India; and in 1774 Hastings was appointed the first Governor-General. He was supported on the Council by his friend and schoolfellow Barwell, while another schoolfellow, Impey, became Chief Justice of the new Supreme Court. But the majority of the Council could out-vote Hastings; and most of the Judges, who came from home, were prejudiced against Anglo-Indians. Revenue continued to fall short; and legal attacks were made upon Hastings by powerful and embittered natives. His position became so difficult that at one time he was forced to send in his provisional resignation; but the Indian Courts found in his favour; and his chief opponent on the Council died, leaving him for the time supreme, though he was still opposed, often factiously, by another colleague, Sir Philip Francis.

In 1777 Imhoff succeeded in obtaining a divorce in Germany; and Hastings then married the Baroness, by whom, however, he had no children. His social position did not suffer in any way from this marriage.

Now in control of his Council, Hastings' foreign policy was to eliminate French power from India and to reduce the principal native leaders to obedience. His generals defeated the armies of the Mahratta princes, Scindia and Holkar, occupied Gujerat and Gwalior, and confirmed the British position in Southern India, where he made a firm alliance with the Nizam of Hyderabad, who had been supported against him by the French Admiral de Suffren at Pondicherry.

In 1781 Barwell, who had been the loyal ally of Hastings, returned to England; and Sir Philip Francis, despite his promises to the contrary, renewed his opposition to the Governor-General, who had only a casting vote in Council when the numbers on a division were equal. Tired of this constant hostility which hampered important measures, Hastings at last provoked Francis to a duel (17th August 1781) and wounded him dangerously; and shortly afterwards Francis returned to England, his avowed enemy. Free again from opposition, Hastings attacked the Rajah of Benares for breaches of various engagements. At first his forces were insufficient and he was obliged to retire from the city, but with reinforcements he succeeded in taking it, and he then laid a heavy indemnity on the Rajah and on his ally the Queen Mother or Begum of Oudh. Hastings thus had his western frontier buttressed against the Mahratta princes by a ring of Mohammedan states; and the Company now in effect filled the position of the old Mogul Emperor, and became the paramount power in India.

But Hastings did not concern himself only with warfare. He started a comprehensive survey of the peninsula, founded the Asiatic Society of Bengal, and set up a college for the education of natives. He also continued his financial reforms, and laid the foundations of an organised Civil Service. At the end of 1784, after ten years' incessant work, he resigned his post.

He arrived in England in June 1785 with about £80,000, a moderate amount considering the opportunities he had had of building up a fortune. He found that Francis had stirred up considerable opposition to him in Parliament and at the India House, and had also enlisted the powerful support of Edmund Burke, who regarded India as a sanguinary, corrupt and enslaved land whose British rulers were fair game for attack. Burke was ready to take exaggerated views and to believe most complaints of interested parties. Indian affairs thus became party politics in England; and for two years the past conduct of Hastings was canvassed in desultory debates in the House of Commons. During this time he received no official recognition, but lived quietly at Windsor, where he occupied himself with a farm and garden. At last, in April 1787, he was regularly impeached by the Commons, and ten months later his trial began in Westminster Hall before the House of Lords. Burke, Fox and Sheridan were among the managers and speakers for the prosecution; but though at first the trial aroused great interest it dragged on for so long that much of this gradually disappeared. Not until seven years later, in April 1795, after the longest public trial on record, was Hastings acquitted. Many addresses and testimonials from India had been adduced in his favour, his personal honesty and "honourable poverty" were never questioned, and his administrative actions, in view of the difficulty of his circumstances, were held to be justified. But the trial had cost him £70,000; and financially he was a ruined man. The directors of the Company properly and generously came to his aid; though he refused the offer of a pension of £2000 a year from the Nawab of Oudh. He had, however, succeeded in buying back for £10,000 his old family home at Daylesford, and there he retired to spend the remainder of his life in country pursuits.

In 1806 Hastings was offered a peerage by the Prince Regent, but he insisted that his impeachment should first be revoked; and to this the Government would not assent. Moira and Wellesley, both future Governors-General of India, stood his friends; and when in 1813 he attended at the Bar of the House of Commons to give evidence about renewing the Charter of the East India Company the whole House stood up and cheered him, as did the House of Lords on the following day. Shortly afterwards he was made a D.C.L. and sworn a member of the Privy Council.

He lived on for some years in the country, taking a lively interest in public affairs, and did not die until August 1818 at the age of eighty-five. He was buried at Daylesford. He left no issue.

Hastings was a scholar and somewhat of a dreamer who set no great value on money, but he was a man of exalted aims and of dogged tenacity and courage. Half of his adult life was spent in India in the centre of affairs of stress and war, and for ten years he was the effective ruler of all the British possessions there. In some ways his code of conduct was lax, but he had a definite policy both in war and peace. He was determined to force his European and native opponents to yield and his English subordinates to be honest, and in both aims he succeeded to a large extent. He it was who really founded the British system of administration and finance in the Indian Empire.

CHARLES EARL CORNWALLIS. 1783.

T. Gainsborough pinx.

CHARLES CORNWALLIS

MARQUESS CORNWALLIS

3

MARQUESS CORNWALLIS

1786-1793 and 1805

CHARLES CORNWALLIS, 2nd Earl and 1st Marquess of that name, was born on 31st December 1738 in Grosvenor Square, London, the eldest son of Charles, 5th Lord and 1st Earl, by Elizabeth, daughter of the 2nd Viscount Townshend, a step-niece of Sir Robert Walpole.

The family of Cornwallis, Irish by origin but long established at Culford in Suffolk, had supported King Charles I during the Rebellion, and at the Restoration had been raised to the peerage. They had also made a number of useful alliances; one of Charles's uncles became Archbishop of Canterbury and his great-uncle had been Prime Minister.

Charles Cornwallis, first styled Viscount Brome, was educated at Eton, where he was fourth in Oppidan Sixth form at the age of sixteen. While at school he received a blow on the eye playing hockey which gave him a squint for life. In 1756 he was commissioned as ensign in the 1st Guards and at once took his profession seriously. After travelling on the Continent with a Prussian officer he studied at the Military Academy at Turin, where he also learned to fence and dance; and when in 1758 his regiment was ordered to the Low Countries he posted off there alone, got himself appointed aide-de-camp to Lord Granby and was present at the battle of Minden. In the following year he was promoted captain in a line regiment, and on coming of age was elected M.P. for his family borough of Eye. He was then made lieutenant-colonel of the 12th Foot, and was engaged in several actions in the campaign of 1762, in

21

which year he succeeded his father as 2nd Earl and took his seat in the House of Lords.

A Whig and a follower of Lords Rockingham and Shelburne, he was now made a Lord of the Bedchamber, an aide-de-camp to the King and a full colonel. He paid some attention to politics, generally supporting the Government, but voted against taxing the American colonies. In 1768, at the age of thirty, he married Jemima, daughter of Colonel James Jones of the 3rd Guards; and a year later, disagreeing with the Government's policy, he resigned his Household post, but was then made Constable of the Tower by George III, who regarded him as a loyal and able officer.

At the age of thirty-six he was promoted major-general, and early in 1776 he was sent to America in command of a division of seven regiments. There, under the command of Sir William Howe, he distinguished himself in several difficult actions. In 1777 he won the battle of Brandywine and occupied Philadelphia. He was then made lieutenant-general and second-in-command of the forces under Sir Henry Clinton; but in the following year he had to return to England because of the illness of his wife, who died shortly afterwards. He went back to America, won the battle of Camden and later took the town of Charleston, where he was one of the storming party; but on 14th October 1781, being unsupported, he was surrounded at Yorktown with 7000 men and had to capitulate to a combined force of French and Americans of three times that size. This defeat put an end to the war; and for three months Cornwallis became a prisoner on parole.

His good reputation, however, and his military ability were recognised by the authorities at home, who knew that he had done his best in unpromising circumstances. He was a favourite both with the King and the Minister; and in the spring of 1782 he was offered the combined Command-in-Chief and Governor-Generalship of India, which he refused as he was still a prisoner on parole. After his release he was sent to Silesia in 1785 on a mission to Frederick the Great, then the greatest soldier of his age; and on his return to England Pitt prevailed on him to accept the Indian appointment, though still against his wish: he took it "with grief at heart."

In the following year Cornwallis set out for India in a stronger position than that of Warren Hastings (for whom he had both friendship and sympathy), for he was to be supreme over his Council in matters of emergency and was also Commander-in-Chief. As a further recognition of his services he was made a Knight of the Garter.

His first task in India was the settlement of the complicated question of the land tenures in Bengal by the local zemindars, who administered the rural revenues on which the whole prosperity of the province depended. In this difficult business he was largely guided by the experience of John Shore, an Indian Civil Servant and one of Hastings' young men, who was later to become Governor-General himself. To give the province security in taxes and tenures a perpetual settlement of assessment was proclaimed; the duties of Revenue Collector and Judge were separated; and Boards of Revenue were instituted. Cornwallis also set up native criminal courts, and made extensive reforms in the civil and military services of the East India Company's establishments—two unpopular changes. Like his predecessors, he was anxious to prevent private trading by the Company's civil employees, and to regulate the relative positions of the officers of the Sepoy and English regiments. He set his face firmly against jobbery and corruption and insisted on decent salaries being paid.

His principal military achievement was the first Mysore war, in which he personally took charge of his army "with great pomp and magnificence." He stormed Bangalore but had to retreat after losing much of his stores and artillery. But in 1791, having secured as allies the Nizam of Hyderabad as well as several Mahratta princes, he defeated Tippoo Sultan and made him surrender some of his territory, hand over two of his sons as hostages, and pay a large indemnity. In a night attack during this campaign Cornwallis was wounded. He gave up his own share of the prize money, nearly £50,000, for the benefit of the Army, with which he always remained a popular hero. He also reduced the French settlement of Pondicherry. For these services he was made a marquess; and in 1793 he resigned his post, which he had held with distinction for nearly seven years.

On his arrival in England early in 1794 the Government made immediate calls on him. He was first sent on a mission to the Continent in an endeavour to get more agreement among the Allies in the war against the French; and on his return, in order to secure the benefit of his military advice, he was appointed Master-General of the Ordnance with a seat in the Cabinet. He kept up his interest in India; there is a letter of his to his successor, Sir John Shore, recommending Colonel "Wesley" (the future Duke of Wellington) of his old regiment as "a good officer." He was then asked to return to India, where matters were not going well; but in 1798 the Government persuaded him instead to take the place of Lord-Lieutenant of Ireland. Pitt said that by accepting this appointment he had conferred a "more essential obligation on his country than any single individual had ever done."

It was a dangerous moment in Ireland. Cornwallis had to keep the country safe from the French, to suppress a domestic rebellion and to force through the unpopular Act of Union by wholesale Government bribery, a method which was extremely distasteful to him; though when the Government demurred to some of his promises to create peers he threatened to resign unless they were fulfilled.

In all these tasks he succeeded. The small French landing party, only 1100 strong, was easily defeated; the Irish Rebellion then collapsed and the hated Act of Union became law. In 1801, after three years in Dublin, he resigned his post, saying that nothing could induce him to serve a Government which continued the old system of proscription and exclusion; for he was a believer in religious toleration. But although he did his work in Ireland with success, he was not much liked. Bishop Percy said of him: "Very civil and pleasant, but will not be a favourite here, for he is very sober himself and does not push the bottle. They also think him too merciful to the rebels."

On his return from Ireland Cornwallis was for a short time put in command of the Eastern District, an important position in view of the threats of invasion from the Continent. Here he complained that "he had neither troops, horses, a house to live in or even an aide-de-camp."

But the Ministry as usual were in need of his services; and he was now sent to Amiens as plenipotentiary to sign the peace treaty with Bonaparte. He had forgotten most of his French and was not much of a diplomat. He had two interviews with Bonaparte, who called him *très dur*; but it was Bonaparte's brother Joseph and Talleyrand who really conducted the negotiations.

Back in England, Cornwallis had some two years' rest, but was then again pressed to return to India as Governor-General in order to bring to an end the expenses and wars incurred by Lord Wellesley. He was now over sixty-six and in failing health; but again a sense of duty forced him to accept. In July 1805 he arrived in Calcutta, and in August started up the Ganges to join the army; the climate, however, was too much for him; he fell ill in September, and on 5th October he died near Benares and was buried at Ghazipor.

The East India Company voted his estate £40,000 in

recognition of his long and distinguished services. His only son, who was for a time Governor of Madras, left no male issue; so the marquessate then expired and the earldom went to his uncle. In the next generation all his titles became extinct.

Cornwallis was essentially a soldier, a man of physical courage and a competent general with a high sense of honour and duty but of quite ordinary abilities. Always trusted by the King and by Pitt, he filled many high and difficult positions with integrity, and though never a statesman he was a brave and honest administrator. In private life he worked hard and lived with simplicity, though in India he entertained sumptuously. Napoleon called him a man of probity and sincerity—*un très brave homme.* His successor in India, Lord Teignmouth, a civilian and a man of peace, who had worked closely with him for many years, had the highest regard for his upright character. Cornwallis was the first English nobleman to govern India, the only man to do so twice, on two Commissions separated by a long interval, and the first ruler who had not lived for many previous years in the country. He was also one of the founders of sound Indian government.

SIR JOHN SHORE

LORD TEIGNMOUTH

4

SIR JOHN SHORE, LORD TEIGNMOUTH

1793-1798

JOHN SHORE, afterwards Lord Teignmouth, was born in St James's Street, London, on 8th October 1751, the son of Thomas Shore of Romford, a supercargo, by Dorothy, daughter of Captain Shepherd, both employees of the East India Company. He came of a Derbyshire family in moderate circumstances. After being educated at Harrow, where Sheridan and Lord Rawdon, afterwards Marquess of Hastings, were his schoolfellows, he was taught book-keeping at Hoxton; and at the age of seventeen he was appointed a clerk in the East India Company's establishment at Calcutta.

First employed in the Secret Service there, he was then sent as assistant to the Revenue Board at Murshidabad, where, owing to his ability, knowledge and industry, he was soon put in charge of a large district, and in 1772 he became first assistant to the Resident at Rajeshahe. By this time he had learnt Persian, the favourite language of the Indian princes, well enough to act as interpreter, and from 1775 to 1780 he was successively a member of the Revenue Council at Calcutta and Revenue Commissioner at Dacca. His attention to revenue and exchequer cases was favourably regarded by Warren Hastings, the Governor-General, until some criticisms which Shore had made on the latter's expenditure forced him to resign his place at the Board, though he retained Hastings' friendship.

In 1786, when on leave in England, Shore married Charlotte Cornish, the daughter of a doctor at Teignmouth, and on his return to India in the following year he was made a member of Council in Bengal. Here his acquaintance with financial affairs and land tenure made him of the highest assistance to Lord Cornwallis in his agricultural and taxation reforms; and he completed a comprehensive review of the whole land settlement for Bengal, Behar and Orissa—his greatest and most permanent work.

When again in England in 1790 he was a witness in favour of Warren Hastings at his trial; and such was now his reputation for knowledge of Indian affairs, particularly in financial matters, that in September 1792 he was created a baronet and appointed Governor-General in succession to Cornwallis; he did not, however, assume his office until the latter's departure from India in the autumn of the following year.

Shore was a pacific and reliable administrator without any territorial ambitions; and his rule in India was characterised by no major events. He was a classical scholar and student of several Eastern languages, but he was concerned with commercial more than with military glory, and he carefully obeyed the injunctions of his masters at the East India Board at home, concentrating on trade and quiet. At times nervous and irresolute, he allowed the Mahrattas and Sikh Rajahs to extend their influence, and he let various native states in the South employ French officers and troops. He dealt gently with a mutiny among his own officers in Bengal; but on the other hand he shewed distinct capacity and courage in settling the intricate question of the succession to the Nawab of Oudh, and so kept the population of that large province at peace.

In 1798, after five years as Governor-General and when not yet fifty years of age, he resigned his post, and on his return home he was created an Irish peer as Lord Teignmouth, though he never took his seat in the Irish House of Lords. Nine years later he was sworn a Privy Councillor and was appointed to the Board of Control in London, where his knowledge of Indian affairs was of real value for many years.

In later life Teignmouth's principal interests were religious, evangelical and philanthropic. With Zachary Macaulay and William Wilberforce he became a leader of the Clapham sect, the suburb in which he lived, and he was the first President of the British and Foreign Bible Society. He was also something of a poet, with literary tastes. He succeeded Sir William Jones, the Persian scholar whose Life he wrote, as President of the Asiatic Society of Bengal. He died in London on 14th February 1834 at the age of eighty-two, leaving a large family. The present Lord Teignmouth is his descendant.

Teignmouth was a competent and industrious official, the third of the four Indian Civil Servants who rose to the post of Governor-General. Macaulay extols his "integrity, humanity and honour"; while his religious enthusiasm, his scholastic attainments and his immense knowledge of Indian land tenure and finance were genuinely respected. Dull and upright, he was neither a great ruler nor a maker of history, but he fulfilled the need of the India Board for a sober and reliable administrator of their Asiatic territories who would bring them peace and large dividends rather than war and large expenses.

J. Pain Davis pinx.

RICHARD WELLESLEY

EARL OF MORNINGTON
MARQUESS WELLESLEY

5

EARL OF MORNINGTON, MARQUESS WELLESLEY

1798-1805

RICHARD COLLEY WELLESLEY was born at Dangan Castle, County Meath, on 20th June 1760, the eldest son of Garrett Wellesley, 2nd Lord Mornington, who a few months later was advanced to an earldom. His mother, the Hon. Anne Hill-Trevor, a daughter of Viscount Dungannon, was a prime figure in the lives of all her children; in later life she used to call herself the mother of the Gracchi. The Wellesley family, though then of no special political account, had been long established in Ireland, where it was noted for its talents: Richard Wellesley's father was an accomplished musician and composer; and Samuel Wesley (the name was variously spelt) was a connection. Of six brothers four became peers, three of whom, Wellington, Wellesley and Cowley, were exceptionally distinguished.

Richard, first called Lord Wellesley, after some schooling at Trim, was sent to Harrow, where he got into trouble for helping to bar out the headmaster. He then went on to Eton, where he shewed remarkable facility in the classics and felicity in verse, tastes that never left him. He made many friends, and at Christ Church did equally well, winning the Chancellor's prize for Latin verse. Just when he came of age his father died; so he did not take a degree, but devoted himself at home in Ireland to paying off debts, putting his estate in order and supervising the education of his younger brothers. Soon after taking his seat in the Irish House of Lords he was elected to a seat in the English House of Commons, where he met his old schoolfellow William Grenville and the latter's cousin, the younger William Pitt. Active and intelligent he was soon made a junior Lord of the Treasury and became a popular member of London society. Some years later he was appointed a member of the Indian Board of Control, and being a friend of Lord Cornwallis, who was recently home from governing India, he paid great attention to Indian affairs. In 1794 he married his mistress Mlle Hyacinthe Gabrielle, daughter of Pierre Roland, whom he had met in the salon of Madame de Genlis in Paris, and by whom he had already had several children.

There had been a talk of Cornwallis returning to India; and in 1797 Mornington was appointed Governor of Madras with the reversion of the Governor-Generalship should it fall vacant. Cornwallis, however, went to Ireland as Lord-Lieutenant; so Mornington took his place as Governor-General of India at the age of thirty-seven, being then given a British barony which he had long coveted.

He arrived in India early in 1798. The political situation was precarious. Tippoo Sultan, the ruler of Mysore, who had recently been defeated at Seringapatam, was again intriguing with the French. There was a strong hostile force in the Deccan; and far away in the North the Afghan ruler of Kabul was known to be preparing for the invasion of India; for the recent policy of Lord Teignmouth had generally been considered weak.

Mornington at once took up the position of a powerful Asiatic potentate with the ceremony and dignity he always was to affect. He was without any military training or commercial knowledge, but he was determined to make the British Raj predominant in India. His younger brother, Arthur Wellesley, Lieutenant-Colonel of the 33rd Foot and already a soldier of some experience and distinction, had been in India for a year, and had made himself well acquainted with the country and its politics. He now became his elder brother's principal military adviser.

"With the arrival of the Wellesleys the whole situation was transformed."

Mornington got himself appointed Captain-General, for he was determined to force matters to a conclusion in Southern India. After a successful campaign in 1799 Tippoo Sultan was defeated and killed; the town of Seringapatam was taken; and the important state of Mysore was brought under British rule, Colonel Wellesley being left there in command of the troops. This campaign finished for the time being the uneasy situation that had so long disturbed Southern India, and put the India House in London and the British Government at ease from its fears of the young Bonaparte's Asiatic ambitions.

In recognition of his successful policy Mornington was made an Irish marquess, which he told Pitt he did not consider an adequate reward; he called it "a double gilt potato." He took the title of Marquess Wellesley, but declined a gift of £100,000 offered him by the directors of the East India Company, though he accepted some of Tippoo Sultan's diamonds. In the meantime he had arranged for the building of a dignified home for the Governor-General in Calcutta in place of the antiquated Fort William. The new palace was built on the model of Adam's Kedleston Hall in Derbyshire, the home of the Curzons. It was to house the rulers of India for over a century.

Southern India being pacified, Wellesley next determined to reduce the powerful Mahratta princes to obedience. The chiefs of these, Scindia of Gwalior, Holkar of Indore and the Peshwa of Poona, were often at loggerheads among themselves. Wellesley worked on a definite plan of *divide et impera*, and after confirming British predominance in Oudh by the Treaty of Lucknow in 1801 he forced the Peshwa to surrender and then directed all his efforts against the other two. General Lake, who commanded in the North, took Delhi and Agra, and the old Mogul Emperor had to ask for British protection; at

C 33

Assaye Arthur Wellesley beat Scindia ; and in 1804 Holkar was subdued; but the expenses of the war increased so much that the directors in London began to find their Governor-General and his soldier brother too costly. Wellesley was recalled; and in 1805 Lord Cornwallis was sent out to relieve him; but he died shortly after his arrival.

Wellesley, however, had achieved much of his plan. The Madras Presidency was almost in its present state; much of Central India had been acquired; and the North-West Provinces were safely under British rule; only the Presidency of Bombay was not yet in complete control. The East India Company, however, determined to finish the war; and Sir George Barlow, who now took over the administration temporarily, obeyed his masters in London.

Wellesley arrived in England early in 1806 to find that his friend Pitt was dying—one of Pitt's last letters asks him to come and see him at Putney. Almost at once, like other retiring rulers of India, he was attacked in Parliament ; but the House of Commons approved generally of what he had done. About this time he was separated from his wife, who had not accompanied him to India.

After speaking once or twice in the House of Lords Wellesley was sent in 1809 as Ambassador to Spain to consolidate the resistance to Napoleon; his brother Sir Arthur Wellesley, now home from India, had been given command of the troops in the Peninsula.

In the summer of that year George Canning resigned the Foreign Secretaryship, and Wellesley was appointed in his place. But he did not get on with his colleagues in the Cabinet. For seven years he had been an Eastern autocrat, and it was not easy to adapt himself to a less prominent position. Lord Grey called him the Atlas of a falling state. Wellesley was also much dissatisfied with the limited supplies and reinforcements sent out to his brother. In 1811 he was concerned with the Prince Regent in negotiations for the formation of a new Government, and was regarded by some as a possible Prime Minister; but his efforts came to nothing; and in the following year he resigned his post. He refused the Lord-Lieutenancy of Ireland but was given the Garter.

In May 1812, on the assassination of Perceval, Wellesley was commissioned to form a government, but he could not succeed in bringing his friends together because, as he said. "of the most dreadful personal animosities." Lord Liverpool. however, was able to make up a ministry which lasted for fifteen years; and in this Wellesley had no place. He was now quite overshadowed by his brother, who was soon to be Duke of Wellington and to whose political views he was strongly opposed. Wellesley was a free trader, in favour of toleration for Roman Catholics, for a policy of retrenchment and reform (the opposite to his views in India), and even against continuing the war with Napoleon, while Wellington held diametrically opposite views.

On the death of George III in 1820 some of the Whigs were admitted to the Government; and Wellesley, now sixty years of age, at last accepted the Lord-Lieutenancy of Ireland. His appointment was at first welcomed there; but local conditions made his task difficult: he was perhaps too vague and philanthropic for the part. Ireland was full of secret societies, faction and smothered rebellion, while many of the Lord-Lieutenant's own subordinates disagreed with his views.

Wellesley had lost his wife in 1816, and in 1825 he married Mrs Marianne Patterson, a daughter of Richard Caton of Baltimore. She was a wealthy American Roman Catholic, a sister of the Duchess of Leeds and socially a great help to her husband; the marriage was in every way happy. In 1828, on Wellington becoming Prime Minister, Wellesley resigned his Irish post, though a few months later the Roman Catholic Relief Acts were adopted by Wellington's own Cabinet. The two brothers were still politically opposed; and not until ten years later was the rift healed; though Wellington always used to say that one of the greatest honours of his life was to be Lord Wellesley's brother.

Wellesley supported the Reform Bill, and in 1832 he was appointed Lord Steward of the Household. He was afterwards again Lord-Lieutenant of Ireland until 1834, when Lord Grey's Government fell. On its return to office in the following year he was for a month Lord Chamberlain, and then finally retired from active life at the age of seventy-four. He had held several expensive posts and by now his means were much embarrassed; so in 1837 he was voted £20,000, which was placed in trust for his use by the East India directors. He lived at Kingston House, Brompton, and mainly occupied himself with classical studies. He died there on 26th September 1842 and was buried at his earliest love, Eton College. Six hundred of the boys followed him to his grave. He left no legitimate issue.

Wellesley was a slight man of no great height but with good looks, a fine voice and an air of authority. Devoted to pleasure even in his later years and very popular with women, he was also a well-read scholar, humorous and of really enlightened views. Though a Whig by education, he had acquired in India an autocratic outlook with a very high idea of his own merits and position; he was constantly resigning his offices and was seldom an easy colleague. In the Peninsular War he loyally supported his brother, and in domestic politics he was equally loyal to his lifelong Liberal principles, though he used to be styled a "sultanised Englishman." Dalhousie called him " indolent to the last degree unless when compelled; and then he was wonderful as a man of business." One of the greatest proconsuls in India, he had a large share in building up the British Empire there by his campaigns and a system of alliances, in rooting out French influence and in converting the East India Company from a mere trading concern into an Imperial and political power.

J. Atkinson pinx.

GILBERT ELLIOT

EARL OF MINTO

6

EARL OF MINTO

1807-1813

GILBERT ELLIOT, afterwards 1st Earl of Minto, was born at Minto in Roxburghshire on 23rd April 1751, the eldest son of Sir Gilbert Elliot, 3rd baronet, by Agnes, daughter of Hugh Dalrymple-Murray-Kynynmound. His grandfather and great-grandfather had both been Scottish judges, bearing the courtesy title of Lord Minto; while his grandmother was a daughter of William Robertson the historian.

As a boy Elliot was taught at the Pension Militaire in Fontainebleau, where Mirabeau was one of his school-fellows; while David Hume, who was then living in Paris, acted as his guardian. He went on to Christ Church as a gentleman commoner, and after spending some time on the Continent he was called to the Bar at Lincoln's Inn in 1774. On the Northern Circuit he got a little practice, and in 1776 was elected to Parliament as a Whig, sitting first for Morpeth and later for Roxburghshire. At first he supported Lord North, but later Fox.

In 1777 he married Anna Maria, daughter of Sir George Amyand, of a rich Huguenot family. He became a friend of Edmund Burke, and collaborated with him in the impeachment of Warren Hastings and Sir Elijah Impey, making several long speeches which raised his forensic reputation. In the House of Commons he was twice proposed as Speaker, against Grenville and Addington respectively, but was beaten on each occasion.

In Parliament he opposed the French Revolution, his knowledge of France being of value. He thus acquired a reputation for statesmanship, and in 1793 was sent out as

Civil Commissioner at Toulon, being then sworn a Privy Councillor and made a D.C.L. of Oxford. From Toulon he went on to Italy, and after some unsuccessful attempts to raise the North Italian states against France he assumed the protectorate of Corsica in 1794. There the British Government gave him a commission to represent them; and for some months he governed the island through a Parliament, with Pozzo de Borgo as his Prime Minister. He also exercised a general control over the British fleet in the Mediterranean; and it was by his direction that Nelson seized the island of Elba. Nelson had a firm belief in him and wrote to him: "I have reserved a place for you on board the *Minerva*. I long to see you, for your advice is a treasure." Elliot was present at the battle of St Vincent in a frigate.

In October 1796 Elliot was ordered to withdraw from Corsica, and he then proceeded to Naples, where he remained until 1798. On his return to England after this romantic adventure he was raised to the peerage as Lord Minto and was elected an F.R.S. A year later he was sent to Vienna as British envoy, and there concluded a treaty of alliance against the French with the Emperor Francis.

In 1806, when Grenville's ministry of All the Talents was formed, Minto was made President of the Board of Control, and a year later he was appointed Governor-General of India on the sudden death of Cornwallis.

He was now a man of fifty-six with considerable administrative experience. He already had some connections in India, for his brother Alexander had been a writer in the East India Company's service and private secretary to Warren Hastings, while another brother was later Governor of Madras. Minto arrived in Calcutta, where Sir George Barlow had been administering the Government, in the summer of 1807 and was soon fully occupied in putting the Indian finances in order. He also devoted himself to ensuring that the various native religions should have complete toleration. Under his aegis native education was developed and several Mohammedan colleges were established. He suppressed the freebooters in Bundelkund and Hariana, and concerned himself particularly with preparing for any possible attacks by Napoleon from the West, sending successive missions to Persia, Afghanistan and the Punjab, none of which, however, were very successful. He also made treaties with Ranjit Singh and the rulers of Sind.

Restricted by his orders from waging war by land, he paid particular attention to India's sea frontiers, suppressing dacoits in the Persian Gulf and annexing the Malacca Islands and Mauritius. In 1811 he seized the island of Java, going there in person with the expedition. The discomforts of this campaign much injured his health. Although, or perhaps because, he had acted with vigour in securing internal order, early in 1813 he was suddenly recalled—it was said in order to make room for Lord Moira, one of the Regent's friends who was financially embarrassed; and he was then created an earl. Well over sixty, and still suffering from the effects of the Java expedition, he arrived in England in May 1814, and a month later died of a chill and strangury at Stevenage while on his way to Scotland. He was buried in Westminster Abbey. He left several children; his great-grandson, the 4th Earl, was Viceroy of India just a century later.

An active and ambitious man, with considerable scholastic and literary tastes, Minto was a discerning politician and diplomat and an energetic administrator. Born of a line of Scottish lawyers, he had had a Continental education, good Parliamentary experience and a sufficient facility in speaking and debate. With plenty of influential friends his undoubted abilities justified the support they gave him. He did well in India, putting its finances in order and devoting himself to extending and strengthening British influence, more by peaceful than by aggressive methods. An energetic patriot at a momentous time, he set a sound and useful example to his successors in office. He was the first of the six Scots who were to rule India and a good example of sober industry and adventure.

T. Gainsborough pinx.

FRANCIS RAWDON

EARL OF MOIRA
MARQUESS OF HASTINGS

7

EARL OF MOIRA, MARQUESS OF HASTINGS

1814-1823

FRANCIS RAWDON, afterwards Earl of Moira and Marquess of Hastings, was born in Dublin on 9th December 1754, the eldest son of John, 1st Lord Rawdon, who seven years later was created Earl of Moira, both in the peerage of Ireland. His mother was Lady Elizabeth Hastings, eldest daughter of Theophilus, 9th Earl of Huntingdon, and later senior co-heiress to several of his baronies.

The Rawdons, originally an old Yorkshire family of some fortune, were later established in County Down. Francis, styled from his eighth year Lord Rawdon, was educated at Harrow and University College, Oxford, and at the age of seventeen was gazetted an ensign in the 15th Foot. Two years later he went off to the American War, where he distinguished himself at the battles of Bunker's Hill and Brooklyn. By 1778 he was a lieutenant-colonel and in that year he was made Adjutant-General to the British Expeditionary Force, Lord Cornwallis having a high opinion of him as a soldier. At the battle of Camden Rawdon commanded a portion of the Army; but in 1781 his health broke down, and on his way back to England he was captured by the French at sea, but was soon released on parole.

During his absence he had been elected to the Irish House of Commons. He had had the reputation of a stern commander in America, and he was now accused by the Duke of Richmond in the House of Lords in London of undue severity. Rawdon insisted on an apology, which he got, and shortly afterwards he was appointed an aide-de-camp to the King and promoted full colonel; early in 1783 he was given a British peerage as Lord Rawdon.

He took some part in politics, siding at first with Pitt, but afterwards joining the Opposition, and he then became a close friend of the Prince of Wales and made some social figure in London. In 1789 he acted as second to the Duke of York in his duel with Colonel Lennox. In that year his maternal uncle Lord Huntingdon died, and his mother inherited her brother's property; and in 1793 Rawdon succeeded his father as Earl of Moira. Being promoted major-general, he was given command of a division of 10,000 men for a secret raid on Brittany to support the French royalists. It proved abortive; but some months later he was sent to the Low Countries to support the Duke of York. While there he made a remarkable and successful forced march from Ostend to Alost, of which the Austrian commander said to him, "*Vous, milord, avez su faire l'impossible.*" For a short time Moira held the Brussels-Antwerp canal, but eventually he had to retreat on Malines.

On his return to England he was again active in Parliament, both in London and Dublin, constantly attacking the Irish administration. Gillray caricatured him as "Lord Longbow, the Alarmist." He took himself very seriously as a politician, and even stated that a number of M.P.s wished him to become Prime Minister instead of Pitt or Fox. On hearing this, Cornwallis, his old commander, said that "excess of vanity and self-importance must have extinguished his understanding, though he once had sense."

In 1798 Moira was promoted lieutenant-general and was later appointed to the command in Scotland, where he became very popular, being elected Grand Master of the Scottish Freemasons; five years later he became a full general. In 1804, in his fiftieth year, he married Flora, only daughter of the 5th Earl, and Countess of Loudoun in her own right.

On the formation of Lord Grenville's ministry in 1806 Moira was appointed Master of the Ordnance and Constable of the Tower, and was sworn of the Privy Council. When his mother died two years later he succeeded to her baronies and fortune. He was still very friendly with the Prince of Wales, supporting him on the Regency question and in his quarrels with his wife, and probably lending him money, for he was a generous and lavish man.

In 1812, after Perceval's assassination and Wellesley's failure to form a Government, Moira was given the same task, but with the same result. In the following year he received the Garter and was appointed Governor-General and Commander-in-Chief in India in place of Lord Minto, a post that was very welcome to him financially. Lord Minto had not left on his arrival, and for some weeks they both lived in Calcutta, though in different houses.

Moira's first act in India was to declare war on the Gurkhas of Nepal, who had been encroaching on Oudh. Three campaigns were needed to bring these brave mountain fighters to reason; but at last in 1816 they were defeated and a satisfactory treaty was made. For this success Moira was created Marquess of Hastings, taking the name of his mother's family; and votes of thanks were passed to him in both Houses of Parliament.

His next business was to engage the Pindaris, the powerful freebooting Hindu tribes of Central India. Hastings himself took command of part of the Army; in a short campaign the Pindaris with their Mahratta allies were completely broken; and in 1818 treaties were concluded with them. This brought the Bombay Presidency to its present size. For these further victories Hastings was again thanked in Parliament and was given a grant of £60,000 by the East India Company.

Though at first opposed to Wellesley's system of subsidiary alliances with native princes, Hastings afterwards adopted it; and the British dominion was thereby widely extended. The Deccan was annexed and much of Central India was reorganised. In the work of reconstruction and pacification he was largely indebted to a number of able administrators—Metcalfe, Munro, Elphinstone, Malcolm and Ochterlony among them. In Curzon's words, "His policy of extending British supremacy and protection over every available native state" made him one of the foremost architects of modern India.

The later years of Hastings in India were not so fortunate. He embarked on another war with the Mahrattas, against the instructions of the East India directors; and he allowed the Palmer banking firm, one of whose partners was married to his ward, to lend large sums of money to the Nizam of Hyderabad, contrary to an Act of Parliament forbidding such loans. This transaction, inadvertent but indiscreet, caused some scandal; the directors at home censured him; and in consequence he resigned his office in 1823.

Hastings was the first Governor-General publicly to discontinue the Nuzzar or presentation of a nominal tribute to the Mogul Emperor. He was also the first to admit Eurasians to Government House and to allow them the rank of field officers in the Army. It was only in his treatment of the Palmer loan that he erred—due apparently to his complete ignorance of financial affairs, for his probity was never questioned. In public works he was exceptionally energetic, paying great attention to the sanitation of Calcutta, then an unhealthy city, and to the waterway of the Hugli. He also restored the canal which supplied Delhi with fresh water. He had not himself conceived the pacification or the consolidation of India, but he put plans for both into effect, and this was really his greatest work.

When he left India in January 1823 his public name was high; but his private financial affairs were in a very unsatisfactory state. He had always spent on an extravagant scale, lending his country house at Donington in England free to the exiled Bourbon princes, and always entertaining his many friends on a large scale. Wraxall called him "the Timon of the present age whose chivalrous spirit and magnificent temper have completely exhausted a splendid fortune." The Government were aware of his position and offered him the Governorship of Malta; and there he spent the last years of his life. In 1826 a fall from his horse seriously injured him. He was taken for a cruise on H.M.S. *Revenge*, and in the Bay of Naples he died on 28th November 1826, being almost seventy-two years old. He was buried at Loudoun. The East India Company voted another £20,000 for the benefit of his eldest son. Hastings left several children; but in the second generation his male issue failed. He, his father and his son all married heiresses who were peeresses in their own right, so that his grandson held sixteen peerages of England, Scotland, Ireland, Great Britain and the United Kingdom. All of these, except the earldom of Loudoun and the baronies by writ, expired in 1868 on the latter's death— "the King of the Plungers"—at the age of twenty-six.

Tall, upstanding, strong and athletic, with very thick, black whiskers, Hastings was called the ugliest man in England. But this was balanced by his genial and affable manner. He was popular with the Army, kind and attentive to women, well read, dignified, scholarly and polite. He was devoted to his work, energetic and industrious. An ambitious and distinguished soldier with a flair for administration, he was never remarkable for political consistency at home, but in India he left his mark as an honest and effective ruler.

Arthur Devis pinx.

WILLIAM PITT AMHERST

EARL AMHERST

8

EARL AMHERST

1823-1828

WILLIAM PITT AMHERST, afterwards Lord and Earl Amherst, was born in Bath on 14th January 1773, the son of Lieutenant-General William Amherst, who had conquered Newfoundland, by Elizabeth, daughter of Thomas Paterson. His godfather was Lord Chatham, and his uncle was Field-Marshal Lord Amherst, who, after a distinguished military career in Canada, as Governor-General of British North America and as Commander-in-Chief in England, had been created a peer with remainder to his nephew. This nephew, William, having lost his parents as a boy, lived with his uncle at Montreal near Rivermead in Kent, where the Amhersts were old legal gentry.

William Amherst was educated at Westminster and Christ Church, and after leaving Oxford he travelled on the Continent, where he learnt French and Italian. In 1797 at the age of twenty-four he succeeded to his uncle's title and property, and three years later he married Sarah, daughter and co-heiress of Lord Archer and widow of the 5th Earl of Plymouth, whom Amherst had met in Naples.

He was early marked out for Court favour and public employment by his connection as well as by his personal gifts. In 1802 he was made a Lord of the Bedchamber, and from 1809 to 1811 he was British envoy to the Court of Naples, just at the beginning of King "Bomba's" reign. There he acquired a reputation for an intelligent knowledge of foreign affairs, and in 1815 he was sworn a Privy Councillor and selected to take a special mission to Peking in order to obtain redress for the bad treatment by the Chinese mandarins of British merchants of the East India Company. After a long journey to the Far East, in Canton and again in Tientsin every effort was made to delude and put Amherst in a position of inferiority, and particularly to make him kowtow to the Manchu Emperor. This he steadfastly refused to do, despite all the endeavours of the mandarins; and in consequence he was forced to return to England without having effected anything but keep his dignity. He travelled back to Canton overland; and, after having been wrecked on his sea journey, at last arrived home in 1817. On his way he visited Napoleon at St Helena and found that the ex-Emperor knew all about his past career. The Government gave Amherst credit for his wise conduct in China; and in 1823, on the retirement of Lord Hastings, he was appointed Governor-General of India. George Canning had been offered the post and Lord William Bentinck had been a candidate for it.

In India Amherst soon found himself involved in a war in Burma with the King of Ava, who had claimed the cession of East Bengal and even tried to attack it. Amherst sent against him one expedition up the Bramaputra into Assam, another by land to Arakan, and a third by sea into the mouth of the Irawadi near Rangoon. The campaign lasted for two years, cost 20,000 lives and £14,000,000; but the King of Ava was eventually defeated, and in 1826 he ceded the maritime provinces of Arakan and Tenasserim. In the meantime Amherst had had to send a force against Bhurtpur in Central India, where the young Rajah who was the British nominee had been driven out by a rival. The city had long been deemed impregnable, but it was carried by assault and the Rajah was reinstated. This victory greatly enhanced the British name in India.

Besides his military expeditions, Amherst had the constant struggle of making the land revenue in India pay for its administration, and also of satisfying the regular demands of the directors of the Company at home for economies and dividends. Another difficulty he had to deal with was a mutiny of Sepoys at Barrackpur caused by their religious fear of crossing the sea. At Barrackpur, about sixteen miles from Calcutta, was the country house of the Governor-General. It was in Amherst's time that Simla was first chosen as the Indian Government's summer station. Lady Amherst's diary gives an interesting account of much of his time in India. The Indian ladies were appalled at the white complexions of her family.

In 1826 Amherst, who had recently lost his eldest son, was advanced to an earldom, and in the following year he resigned owing to failing health, though only fifty-four.

On returning to England he was given his old place in the Royal Household, and in 1835 he was nominated Governor-General of Canada; but his appointment was cancelled by the incoming Whig Government. In 1838 his wife died; and a year later, at the age of sixty-six, he married another Countess of Plymouth, widow of the 6th Earl. She was a daughter of John Sackville, 3rd Duke of Dorset, Amherst's friend and neighbour at Knole, which she later inherited from her brother. There Amherst, who had long retired from public life, died on 13th May 1857 at the age of eighty-four, having been alive with twenty-four of his predecessors and successors as Governors-General. He left a large family by his first wife. The present earl is his descendant.

Amherst was an honest, straightforward man, raised in a good school, a capable and courageous administrator, but an inconspicuous Governor-General. His early diplomatic experience enabled him on more than one occasion to compose difficult cases in China and India; and his hereditary military instincts were of value in directing warfare. A reliable ruler without too much talent or ambition, he was an example of training, duty and tradition.

Sir T. Lawrence pinx.

LORD WILLIAM BENTINCK

9

LORD WILLIAM BENTINCK

1828-1835

L ORD WILLIAM CAVENDISH-BENTINCK was born
on 14th September 1774, the second son of William
Henry, 3rd Duke of Portland, and Lady Dorothy Cavendish,
daughter of the 4th Duke of Devonshire. His father and
his maternal grandfather were the heads of two of the chief
Whig families and had both been Prime Ministers; he
thus began his career under promising auspices.

At the age of seventeen he was gazetted an ensign in
the Coldstream Guards; in the following year he was
promoted to a troop in a Dragoon regiment, and in 1794,
before he had come of age, he was a lieutenant-colonel
serving as A.D.C. to the Duke of York in the Low Countries.
At twenty-two he was elected M.P. for Camelford, a seat
he subsequently exchanged for Nottinghamshire. In 1799
he was again abroad, serving successively at the headquarters of the Russian and Austrian armies and being
present at a number of battles against the French, including Marengo, the Mincio and the Adige.

In 1803 he married Lady Mary Acheson, daughter of
Arthur, 1st Earl of Gosford, and in that year he was
appointed Governor of Madras while still under thirty.
The Presidency was not yet at peace after the Mysore
war with Tippoo Sultan; and the land question was in
process of settlement. Bentinck was against the institu-
tion of zemindars or large feudal proprietors as it obtained
in Bengal, preferring the system of ryot or peasant culti-
vators recommended by some of his subordinates. While
this important matter was in dispute a serious mutiny
broke out in Vellore among the Sepoy regiments, who had

51

been forbidden by the British military authorities to wear their beards, turbans and caste marks when in uniform. A number of British officers and troops were killed; and the India House directors, placing the responsibility for this on Bentinck, in 1807 recalled both him and his Commander-in-Chief. It seems that Bentinck was really free from blame, but he had to take the responsibility. He greatly resented this treatment.

The Duke of Portland, a man of seventy, had just then become Prime Minister for the second time; and a few months after his return to England Bentinck, now a major-general, was sent out to the Peninsular War, first to serve on the staff of Sir Harry Burrard in Portugal and later on a mission to the Spanish Junta. He subsequently commanded a brigade under Sir John Moore, and then, as a lieutenant-general, was given a division in Sir Arthur Wellesley's army.

In 1811 he was sent as Envoy to Sicily with the command of the British troops in that island; and there he remained on and off until 1814, acting really as Governor and even promulgating a constitution. For a time he also commanded a division in Eastern Spain, where he was defeated at Ordal by Marshal Suchet. Wellington had no great opinion of his military abilities; and after the end of the war Bentinck, having received a G.C.B. and other decorations, lived in Rome, where he remained without employment for ten years. The question of his return to India was raised more than once; but he was still held to be too impetuous and inexperienced, though James Mill, who had great influence at the India Office, thought him the best candidate. It was to Mill that Bentinck once said: "What I have read amounts to very little, and it is not without pains that I can read anything."

But in July 1827 Canning suddenly appointed him Governor-General of India in succession to Lord Amherst. Canning was an old friend, connection and supporter of the Duke of Portland; he had himself been President of the Board of Control and had been offered the Governor-Generalship some years previously; while Bentinck's long, varied and not undistinguished record of service as a soldier, administrator and politician seemed to justify the appointment. Bentinck was sworn of the Privy Council, and in the following year he assumed his office.

His seven years' rule of India, though not marked by any great victories or accessions of territory, were distinguished by memorable advances in justice and administration. Following the Burmese War there had latterly been an annual deficit of £1,000,000 in the Indian Budget. By reduction of expenditure, increased revenue from unassessed lands and a tax on opium Bentinck converted this into a surplus of double that amount. In the face of widespread native opposition he abolished suttee, the Hindu widow-burning religious ceremony which was a barbarous relic of bygone ages—and he put down the thugs or paid assassins, a brotherhood of stranglers who covered the country. With wide toleration he admitted natives to many posts in the public service, allowed any Europeans to live in India, and initiated the freedom of the Press. In these reforms Macaulay, the first Law member of Council in India, and Mill at home were largely his advisers. Sir William Hunter says: "The modern history of the British in India ruling the country as benevolent administrators with an eye to the good of the natives begins with Bentinck."

It was in 1833, during Bentinck's term of office, that the Charter of the East India Company was renewed for another twenty years; by this Act the old title of Governor-General of Bengal was altered to that of Governor-General of India; the Chinese trade was also thrown open to all.

Bentinck's diplomatic and political work also included treaties with the Amirs of the Punjab and of Sind, and the taking over of the administration of Coorg and Mysore. He considerably developed the facilities in India for general education, making English the official language of the Peninsula—a salient feature of his administration. It thus became the vernacular of the educated classes, who often could not converse with each other in their own tongues; and in time it fostered the movement towards nationalism. Bentinck had a love of work and was a great writer of minutes on nearly every subject.

By 1834 his health had worsened, and in March 1835 he returned to England. He declined a peerage, but was elected M.P. for Glasgow as a Liberal, though he took little part in politics. On 17th June 1839 he died in Paris, leaving no issue.

Bentinck was a man of exemplary private life who devoted himself to the service of his country for no material reward. Of the highest birth and connection though of no particular intellectual ability, he had acquired by long and varied experience a wide knowledge of government which he exercised with a broad and benevolent mind. His administration has always been regarded as a turning-point in the methods of British rule in India, for it recognised that India should be governed for the benefit of the Indians. He was a good type of the comparatively uneducated aristocrat whose traditions, high ideals, industry and energy made him an invaluable public servant. Absolutely honest in intentions and patronage, magnificently hospitable, he was said never to have taken any important step without consulting his wife. Her portrait is the only one of a Governor-General's wife that hung on the walls of Government House, Calcutta.

L. *Dickinson pinx.*   *J. Thompson s*

GEORGE EDEN

EARL OF AUCKLAND

10

EARL OF AUCKLAND

1835-1842

GEORGE EDEN, afterwards Lord and Earl of Auckland, was born at Eden Farm, Beckenham, on 25th August 1784, the second son of William Eden, 1st Lord Auckland, by Eleanor, daughter of Sir Gilbert Elliot and sister of the 1st Earl of Minto. His father, son of a North-country baronet of old family and a close friend of the younger Pitt (his eldest daughter had been Pitt's first and only love), had sat in the House of Commons for many years and had been made first an Irish and then a British peer, after filling with ability a number of political and diplomatic posts—though equally famous for his political tergiversations.

George Eden was educated at Eton and Christ Church, and in 1808 was called to the Bar and nominated Deputy Teller of the Exchequer, a comfortable sinecure. When he was twenty-five his elder brother was drowned; and Eden succeeded to his seat for Woodstock and sat for four years in the House of Commons as a Whig. In 1810 his father died, and he took his seat in the House of Lords. His uncle Lord Minto, a distinguished diplomat, had recently been appointed Governor-General of India; and his nephew regarded his example with respect.

Auckland, who never married, took his Parliamentary duties seriously, attending the House regularly and making solid and sensible speeches; and after twenty years of this loyal support, in 1830 he was taken by Lord Grey into his Cabinet as President of the Board of Trade. This was the first executive office he held, at the age of forty-five. Four years later Lord Melbourne made him

First Lord of the Admiralty, and in 1835 Governor-General of India to succeed Lord William Bentinck. Since the latter's retirement the Government had been administered by Sir Charles Metcalfe, a Civil Servant of great eminence and experience whom the directors had indeed wished to succeed him.

Nothing of special importance was occupying the Indian scene at the moment. Auckland carried on quietly and did good work in the famine of 1838, visiting the affected areas and setting up relief camps. As he was a bachelor his two sisters, who idolised him, acted as hostesses for him. Their journals and letters are well known.

By this time the North-West Frontier question had begun to bulk largely in British policy. Auckland knew his uncle, Lord Minto's, political views, and, fearing the machinations of Russia in Central Asia, soon turned his attention to Afghanistan. There were two claimants to the Afghan throne, Shah Shuja, who was the British candidate, and his cousin Dost Mohammed. The latter seized it; and after some unsuccessful negotiations in 1838 Auckland sent an army of 20,000 men under Sir John Keane through Sind into the country who took Kandahar and Ghazni and later on Kabul: the expedition indeed was called "the military promenade." Shah Shuja was then proclaimed Amir; and Dost Mohammed fled to the North.

All this news was at first so favourable that in 1839 Auckland was given an earldom. But many misfortunes were to follow an apparently successful campaign which the East India directors at home had deprecated. Two British political agents with a body of British and native troops had been left in Afghanistan. Against these Dost Mohammed's son, Akbar Khan, raised an insurrection; the British agents were treacherously killed, and some British officers and ladies imprisoned; while the Anglo-Indian force was besieged and starved in its cantonments, until eventually it had to capitulate. This was the first Afghan War. Not until January 1842 did the Afghans at last allow the British troops to set out on their return march to India; but no provisions were supplied, the winter season was exceptionally severe, and they were attacked and harassed on all sides by tribesmen, so that at last out of 16,000 men only one escaped. Six months later another expedition under General Pollock advanced on Kabul, routed the Afghans and rescued the British prisoners, restoring to some extent British prestige. But in the meantime Auckland had been recalled; the reprisals took place under his successor.

While in India, he had shewn some attention to native education and to the progress of medicine, founding various Government scholarships for these purposes. Macaulay, who was President of the Committee of Public Instruction, had inspired much of this work.

Some years after his return to England Auckland was again made First Lord of the Admiralty in Lord John Russell's Cabinet; but his career was finished; his health had suffered severely in India, and on 1st January 1849 he died suddenly at Alresford. As he had never married, his earldom became extinct: his brother Robert, Bishop of Sodor and Man and later of Bath and Wells, succeeded to his minor titles.

Auckland was a loyal party man, a steadfast supporter of Reform and a sufficiently capable politician and assiduous official in normal times; but he was diffident, without experience in affairs of action, vacillating and quite ignorant of the East. A prey to Russophobia and anxious to emulate his uncle in defending India against possible future dangers, he acted precipitately, induced a crisis which probably need not have occurred, and did not shew any great talent in dealing with it. He was one of the least distinguished of those who have held his place. Creevey calls him "a notorious and useless jobber";

but Greville says, "A man without shining qualities or strong accomplishments, austere and almost forbidding in his manner, silent and reserved, unpretending in public and private life, but nevertheless universally liked; placid, modest, cheerful, with good taste and understanding, benevolent and affectionate; his life was useful, honourable and prosperous, his memory honoured and regretted."

F. R. Say pinx.

EDWARD LAW

EARL OF ELLENBOROUGH

11

EARL OF ELLENBOROUGH

1842-1844

EDWARD LAW, afterwards Lord and Earl of Ellenborough, was born on 8th September 1790, the eldest son of Edward Law, later 1st Lord Ellenborough and Lord Chief Justice of the Common Pleas, by Ann, daughter of Captain George Towry, R.N., of Shipley, Northumberland. The Laws were an old stock of yeomen in Westmorland who became distinguished for their ability in the Church and the Law. Edmund, the grandfather, was Bishop of Carlisle; and one of his sons was Bishop of Bath and Wells, while one of the Chief Justice's sons was Recorder of London.

Edward Law was educated at Eton and at St John's College, Cambridge, where he was the author of a prize poem. He had wished to be a soldier, but to please his father (who gave him the lucrative place of Chief Clerk of the Common Pleas, which he held for twenty-six years) he became in 1813 M.P. for St Michael's in Cornwall, and in the same year married Lady Octavia Stewart, younger daughter of the 1st Marquess of Londonderry and sister of Lord Castlereagh, the Foreign Secretary. With the latter Law became friendly at the Congress of Vienna; and from 1818, when he succeeded his father, he took an active part in Parliament in opposition to Canning's policy. He also interested himself in military matters and spoke well on foreign affairs.

In 1819 he lost his wife, and five years later he married Jane Elizabeth, daughter of Sir Henry Digby and granddaughter of Tom Coke of Holkham, 1st Earl of Leicester. Known as "Aurora, the Light of Day," she was a woman of remarkable beauty and intelligence, an artist, with delightful manners and fascination—but also of somewhat casual virtue.

In 1828, when Wellington's Government was formed, Ellenborough was sworn of the Privy Council, given the sinecure post of Lord Privy Seal, and later that of President of the Board of Control. Here he made himself thoroughly conversant with the position in India and took an unusually prominent part in shaping Indian policy, going in and out with the Tory Governments during the next few years. In 1830 he divorced his wife for adultery with Prince von Schwartzenburg, with whom he fought a duel, receiving also £25,000 damages. She afterwards became mistress of the King of Bavaria and later married Baron von Venningen, his Prime Minister, who committed suicide when she deserted him. Her third husband was an Arab general named Sklikh with whom she lived in Damascus, where she died at the age of seventy-four.

Ellenborough had always maintained an assiduous and rather bellicose attention to Indian affairs, more particularly in relation to possible Russian aggression; and in 1841, when he was again President of the Board of Control, Sir Robert Peel offered him the post of Governor-General to replace Lord Auckland and clear up the position in Afghanistan. This post he gladly accepted, and he arrived in Madras early in the following year.

He had intended, so he had told the East India directors, to restore peace to Asia—a policy of quiet trade expansion. His first act was to compose a mutiny among the Sepoys; and his second to improve the measures and increase the reinforcements for the Chinese War, which was eventually brought to a successful conclusion. Military affairs always attracted him; and the situation in Afghanistan left by Auckland impelled him only to terminate hostilities when a victory had been achieved, which to some extent restored British prestige. He gave his commands "in well-chosen

words which left his generals responsible for any disaster."
Their successes he celebrated by grandiose parades of
elephants and bombastic proclamations to the princes,
which were the object of much ridicule all over India.
He prepared his despatches with his own hand, being justly
proud of his own peculiar style.

In 1843 he embarked on another war against the Amirs
of Sind, where Sir Charles Napier with 3000 British
troops defeated 20,000 Baluchis at Miani. By this victory
Ellenborough was able to secure the reopening of the
waterway of the Indus for trade; and subsequently, on the
excuse that the Amirs had not adhered to their treaties,
he annexed that province and so ensured penetration into
the heart of the Punjab—the occasion of the telegram
"Peccavi"—(I have Sind). This war he followed up by
an attack on Gwalior, where on the death of the reigning
Maharajah the Ranee had tried to place an adopted son
on the throne. In this campaign Ellenborough was himself
present at the battle of Maharajahpore, when the Mahratta
army was defeated and the state of Gwalior taken over.

But despite these victories he had not endeared himself
to the directors at home; he had pursued a policy of
war rather than peace, he had increased rather than
diminished expenditure, he had treated their despatches
with disrespect, and by his favouritism of the Army he had
provoked his Civil Servants. In 1844 he was recalled,
after an eventful two years which had indeed expanded the
limits of Britain's power in India and had certainly
maintained her name. On his return to England he was
made a G.C.B. and created an earl, having already received
the thanks of Parliament for his conduct of the Afghan
campaign.

In 1846 he rejoined the Cabinet of Sir Robert Peel
as First Lord of the Admiralty, but resigned with his
leader a few months later. By this time he had acquired
the reputation of an erratic genius, a man who would

tolerate no control; being, in the words of Queen Victoria, "entirely unable to submit to general rules of conduct." But he was a practised orator, full of knowledge and experience, and a valuable member of his party in opposition. Gladstone told Curzon that Ellenborough was the best speaker of his day in the House of Lords. He spoke strongly against the Crimean War; and in 1858 Lord Derby included him in his Government as President of the Board of Control (for the fourth time). But in this position, by allowing a private letter of rebuke to Lord Canning, then Governor-General of India, to be published in the press, he offended both the Queen and Parliament; and to avoid a vote of censure which might have displaced the Ministry he resigned in June 1850. After this he never held office again, though he went on taking part in debates for another ten years. He died at Southam on 22nd December 1871, leaving no issue; the present Lord Ellenborough is a descendant of his brother.

Ellenborough, like his father, was a man of conspicuous energy and talents, of much industry and information, a powerful speaker and a genuine authority on foreign and military affairs, though, like his father, overbearing and impatient of correction. Pompous and theatrical, and much maligned during his lifetime for his actions in India, it is now generally admitted that on a long view they were right, and that his faults, mostly specious, were more than compensated for by the enduring results of his Indian administration, short and chequered as it was.

HENRY HARDINGE

VISCOUNT HARDINGE

12

VISCOUNT HARDINGE

1844-1848

HENRY HARDINGE, afterwards Viscount Hardinge, was born on 30th March 1785 at Wrotham in Kent, the third son of the Rev. Henry Hardinge, Rector of Stanhope, County Durham, by Frances, daughter of James Best of Boxley in Kent. His family came from King's Norton in Derbyshire, where an ancestor had raised a troop of horse for Charles I and had been knighted at the Restoration. His grandfather was Nicholas Hardinge, Clerk of the House of Commons, who had married Jane, daughter of Sir John Pratt, Chief Justice of the King's Bench.

Henry Hardinge's eldest brother, Charles, succeeded to the baronetcy of an Irish uncle and became a parson like his father; his second brother, George, a captain in the Navy, was killed in 1808 in an action with the French off Ceylon; and his youngest brother, Richard, rose to be a major-general.

Henry himself was educated at Durham, and at the age of fifteen joined the Queen's Rangers in Canada, where he remained until 1804, when he was promoted captain in the 57th Foot. He then entered the Royal Military Academy at High Wycombe as a student, and did so well that he was posted to the Quartermaster-General's staff of Sir Brent Spencer, who went out in command of the Peninsular expedition in 1807.

Hardinge's career in Spain and Portugal was a succession of solid service and dashing exploits. He was wounded at Vimiera and was by the side of Sir John Moore at Corunna. Promoted major on Sir W. Beresford's staff in Portugal, he took part in the battles of Busaco and Badajos and was twice mentioned in despatches.

At Albuera he specially distinguished himself, the timely orders that he gave, largely on his own responsibility, having much to do with the victory. At Vittoria he was again wounded, and by 1814 he was in command of a Portuguese brigade at Toulon.

In 1815, having been twelve times mentioned in despatches for distinguished services, he was knighted, made a K.C.B. and promoted lieutenant-colonel in the Grenadier Guards, all before he was thirty years of age. He was sent to the Congress of Vienna with Sir Charles Stewart, and on the escape of Napoleon from Elba he was attached as liaison officer, with the rank of brigadier-general, to Prince Blücher's staff; the Duke of Wellington had great confidence in his alertness and ability as a staff officer.

At Ligny Hardinge had his left hand shot off, but he remained at his post throughout the action until he was carried to the Prince's headquarters; and when he eventually arrived in an ambulance at the Palais de St Cloud a line of Blücher's guards received him holding torches, and he was put to sleep in the Empress Marie Louise's bed. It was to him that Blücher said, "*Lieber Freund, ich stinke etwas!*" (he had taken medicine). After Waterloo, Wellington devoted a special gazette to Hardinge's services, and later gave him Napoleon's sword to wear; while the King of Prussia decorated him with the Prussian Order of Merit. During these campaigns Hardinge was wounded four times, had four horses shot under him, received four steps in rank and ten foreign decorations.

On returning to England Hardinge entered Parliament, being elected first for Durham and later for St Germans, Newport and Launceston successively. In 1821 he married Lady Emily James, a daughter of the 1st Marquess of Londonderry, and formerly wife of the British Minister in the Netherlands. He thus became a brother-in-law of Castlereagh and Ellenborough.

Two years later he was appointed Clerk of the Ordnance,

and in 1828 he entered the Cabinet as Secretary at War. For a short time in 1830 and 1834 he was Chief Secretary for Ireland, for both Wellington and Peel were his close friends and placed implicit trust in his loyalty and judgment. When he was appointed to Ireland someone asked Wellington whether he was strong enough for the post. The Duke said: "Hardinge will do; he always understands what he undertakes and never undertakes anything he does not understand." Indeed, in all his posts Hardinge was successful both as a statesman and as a speaker. He was known as "the Soldiers' Friend." Many fundamental principles in the organisation of the Army were initiated by him; recruiting, pensions, discipline, finance and armaments being all subjects to which he gave his closest attention. He was also a popular and famous adviser as regards duels, his tact and sense of honour being universally respected.

In 1842 he was offered the Command-in-Chief in India. This he refused; but two years later, at the age of fifty-nine, he accepted the post of Governor-General, in succession to his brother-in-law, Lord Ellenborough.

On his journey out he had an interview with the Khedive of Egypt, and after inspecting Aden he arrived in Calcutta in July 1844. It was known that a war with the Sikhs in the North-West was probable, for their capital at Lahore had been torn with dissensions since the death of their ruler, Ranjit Singh, five years previously; and after the recent British defeats in Afghanistan the Sikh leaders looked forward to easy victories. In 1845 a Sikh army of 60,000 men with 150 guns crossed the Sutlej and invaded British territory. The Commander-in-Chief, Sir Hugh Gough, fought four pitched battles in three weeks and finally defeated the enemy at Sobraon, when Lahore surrendered. This was the first Sikh War. The infant son of Ranjit Singh was then appointed Rajah; and a British force and Resident were quartered in the Punjab. Hardinge himself had taken part in the campaign, insisting on serving under

Gough, though his senior in rank. They had, however, several differences of opinion as to the conduct of the operations, in which Hardinge as Governor-General occasionally overrode (rightly) his Commander-in-Chief. He also gave up his own baggage animals, 300 camels and 60 elephants, to the Army Commissariat. After this campaign Hardinge was raised to the peerage as a viscount and was granted a pension of £3000 a year for life.

The remaining years of his rule in India were quiet and were mainly devoted to public works; the Ganges canal, a civil engineers' college, sanatoria, tea culture and the care of ancient monuments were among the subjects to which he paid special attention.

In 1848, at his own request, he was relieved of his office, being succeeded by Lord Dalhousie; and four years after his return to England, on the death of the Duke of Wellington, he was appointed Commander-in-Chief of the British Army. But for this post he was rather old and perhaps too closely wedded to the former routine; and though he made some useful changes in the organisation of the Army, the outbreak of the Crimean War found it not as up to date as it might have been.

In 1855, at the age of seventy, he was made a Field-Marshal, but in the following year he was attacked by paralysis when attending the Queen at an Aldershot review where he had recently started the permanent military camp. He died at South Park on 24th September 1856. His grandson Charles, Lord Hardinge of Penshurst, was Viceroy of India from 1910 to 1916. The present viscount is his great-grandson.

Hardinge was one of the most gallant of soldiers, able, courageous and hard-working, with a high sense of honour and duty. Though his short term of office in India came late in life, he shewed plenty of strength and breadth of view in his administration there. But it is in the Army, to which he was devoted, that his name is best remembered.

J. W. Gordon pinx.

JAMES RAMSAY

MARQUESS OF DALHOUSIE

13

MARQUESS OF DALHOUSIE

1848-1856

J AMES ANDREW BROUN-RAMSAY, afterwards Earl
and Marquess of Dalhousie, was born at Dalhousie Castle
in Midlothian on 22nd April 1812, the third son of George,
9th earl in the Scots peerage, by Christian, daughter and
heiress of James Broun of Coulston, County Haddington.
His father, of an ancient Lowland family, was a distinguished
soldier who had commanded a division in the Peninsular
War, fought at Waterloo as a lieutenant-general, and in
1815 was made a G.C.B. and given a barony of the United
Kingdom. From 1819 to 1828 he was Governor-General of
Canada, and from 1829 to 1832 Commander-in-Chief in
India. Sir Walter Scott, his schoolfellow and lifelong
friend, called him "always steady, wise and generous," and
his wife "amiable, intelligent and lovely."

James Ramsay passed his childhood in Canada and was
then sent to Harrow. While he was there Lord Hastings,
an old Harrovian and just back from governing India,
came down and gave the boys £2 apiece, an impressive
recollection for them all. Ramsay went on to Christ
Church, where he had as friends W. E. Gladstone, Canning
and Elgin, two of whom were also to be Governors-General
of India. After a tour in Northern Italy, by the death of
his eldest brother in 1832 he became his father's heir and
was then styled Lord Ramsay. In 1835 he contested
Edinburgh against Campbell, a future Lord Chancellor,
and Abercrombie, a future Speaker, but was beaten,
though his vigorous speeches made a good impression.
In the following year he married Lady Susan Hay, daughter
of George, 8th Marquess of Tweeddale, and in 1837 was

67

elected M.P. for Haddington, sitting first as a Conservative and later as a Peelite. But his service in the House of Commons was short, for in 1839 he succeeded his father and took his seat in the House of Lords. For a time he served as Grand Master of Scottish Freemasons, and also as an Elder in the General Assembly of the Church of Scotland; but though he had advanced ideas he would not accept all the proposals of innovations, so he protested and left the Assembly.

In 1843, after Sir Robert Peel became Prime Minister, Dalhousie was made Vice-President of the Board of Trade under his friend Gladstone; and two years later succeeded him as President. It was the time of railway development, and to this he devoted his mind. Though himself in favour of state railways, he adapted his views to the national system of free competition, and during a whole year he examined personally every railway scheme in the country, labouring at his office day and night, his table stacked with plans. He was always a glutton for work.

Before going out of office Peel had made Dalhousie Lord Clerk Register in Scotland, a post worth £1200 a year, which was a welcome addition to his limited income. Lord John Russell, on becoming Premier, offered him a place in the Cabinet, and on his refusing this made him a Knight of the Thistle. But when Russell pressed him to go to India as Governor-General, Dalhousie, with Peel's approval, accepted, and in 1848, at the early age of thirty-five, he arrived in Calcutta, already regarded as a genius.

He at once settled down to the hardest work, making himself master of every detail of administration and never sparing himself; this was always one of his leading traits. "He did an immense amount of work with his own hand in a handwriting singularly neat and clear, with a lucid but caustic style. His speeches were concise and clear and he had a keen sense of the ludicrous." The chief events which marked his eight years' rule in India were the conquest of the Punjab and of Lower Burma, the consolidation of seven native states, and the laying of railways (his *forte*) and telegraphs all over the country. The second Sikh War in 1849 and the capture of the Punjab were really forced upon Dalhousie by the insolence of the Sikhs and the murder of two British officers. After a varying campaign and a Pyrrhic victory at Chillianwalla the Sikhs were finally defeated at Gujerat, and the Punjab annexed, being placed under a Board of which Sir Henry Lawrence was made President. For these successes Dalhousie was thanked by Parliament and created a marquess in 1849.

Two years later the King of Burma's attitude to British merchants became so oppressive and his own Government so tyrannical that after a lapse of a quarter of a century a second Burmese war was begun. Rangoon and Pegu were taken by assault by the British; and Dalhousie, who had himself largely prepared the administrative military work, went to Rangoon and inaugurated the new province of Lower Burma.

His domestic policy was equally fortunate. The succession in several of the feudatory states—Nagpur, Sattra and Jhansi—had latterly given rise to dangerous dynastic disputes; while Oudh for many years had been grossly misgoverned by its native rulers. They were accordingly all taken over by the British Raj, though their annexation was criticised at home. Meanwhile the Governor-General had set up an Indian Public Works Department, had laid a railroad, post and telegraph system over much of the country, and had inaugurated steam communication by sea with England. He also developed irrigation, lowered local taxes, and extended education and civil rights to all classes of the population. So useful and beneficent was his rule that his term of office was twice extended; and it was only when his health had quite broken down in 1856 that he resigned.

He had already lost his wife; and this blow, with his

incessant devotion to work, had gradually turned him from a strong man into a complete invalid.

The East India Company gave him a pension of £5000 a year; but he was unable to take any further part in public life. After his return home he was greatly shattered by the events of the Indian Mutiny and by the many attacks in the press which were made on him; for the neglect of proper military preparations were ascribed to him, though he had always pressed for a better and larger army. On 19th December 1860 he died at Dalhousie; and as he left no son his marquessate expired.

Dalhousie was a slight and small but handsome man. Of a very masterful disposition and somewhat of a theorist he had pronounced views, usually acquired by his own personal study and examination. He was a good judge of character and a loyal friend to his subordinates, but thoroughly conscious of his own power and position. Greville called him "a good man of brains and an excellent speaker"; Broughton thought him "sensible, of good capacity though without much instruction or brilliancy." Less friendly critics held him "vain, despotic, resenting opposition, with little imagination or understanding of Indians." Essentially peaceful, he on more than one occasion overruled his generals on military questions. Had he stuck to political life in England he would almost certainly have gone very high, but he preferred to devote all his energies to the government of India and its people—consolidating its internal states, developing its communications and adding to it four large kingdoms on the East and West. Lord Curzon regarded him as incomparably the greatest administrator who was charged with the destinies of India since Warren Hastings.

CHARLES CANNING

EARL CANNING

14

EARL CANNING

Governor-General and Viceroy (from 1858)
1856-1862

CHARLES JOHN CANNING, afterwards Viscount and Earl Canning, was born at Gloucester Lodge in Brompton on 14th December 1812, the third son of George Canning of Dublin, who had recently been Foreign Secretary and was to become Prime Minister fifteen years later. The Cannings were originally small squires in Garvagh; but George had a younger brother, Stratford, who had become a prosperous merchant; while he himself had married Joan Scott, daughter and co-heiress of General John Scott of Balcomie, another of whose daughters was the wife of the 4th Duke of Portland, son of the Prime Minister.

Charles Canning was educated at Eton, where he acquired some prestige. While he was there his father died after being for a few months Prime Minister. His mother was then created a viscountess, a title to which Charles later became heir by the death of his elder brothers. He went on to Christ Church, where he took a first in classics. Elgin and Dalhousie, also to be Governors-General of India, were his contemporaries.

In his twenty-first year he married Charlotte, daughter of Lord Stewart de Rothesay. She was "perfectly lovely from infancy"; while Canning, like his father, was "singularly handsome, a great gentleman in character and demeanour."

In August 1836 he was elected M.P. for Warwick, and a few months later he succeeded his mother and entered the House of Lords. In 1841 he was made Under-Secretary

71

at the Foreign Office by Sir Robert Peel, and on the latter's resignation in 1846 he was sworn a Privy Councillor. On the Conservatives returning to office Canning was offered by Lord Derby the post of Foreign Secretary; but this for party reasons he felt unable to accept. Next year, however, he became Postmaster-General under Aberdeen, and he continued in that post under Palmerston until in 1855 he was appointed Governor-General of India, a post that had been offered to his father a generation earlier.

He went out full of high hopes, determined to pursue the path of peace, though well aware, as he said, that in the East not even the wisest Government can command it. Almost at once he found himself obliged to declare war on Persia, which was attacking Herat in the west of Afghanistan. The campaign was successfully concluded in a few months; and then suddenly, in May 1857, came the Mutiny.

The Indian Mutiny broke out almost a century after the battle of Plassey (23rd June 1757–10th May 1857). Many causes contributed to it. Lord Dalhousie had recently annexed several native states and dispossessed their ruling dynasties. He had laid up and down the peninsula lines of telegraphs and railways, the strength and value of which were already being realised and feared by the natives; Indians of whatever caste, birth or education were still debarred from all the higher posts in the Army or Civil Service; the Crimean War had left an impression all over India that the English were not invincible; while many Indians believed their own troops to have been largely responsible for the recent conquest of the Punjab. Whether or not any foreign influence was behind the Mutiny is still not known; but there were certainly many discontented Indian princes; there was a belief that the century of English rule was now to come to an end; and there was a general fear among the Sepoys that India was to be christianised. Colour was given to this by a panic talk which ran through the native regiments that some new issues of cartridges were greased with cows' or pigs' fat, sacred or unclean animals respectively to Hindus and Muslims. In this tale there was some truth; and with sufficient fuel to hand the spark was sufficient to set it alight.

The Mutiny began at Meerut, the largest military station in Northern India. On a Sunday afternoon in May a Sepoy regiment mutinied against their British officers. No sufficient action was taken at once; and next morning Delhi followed suit. At Delhi there were large stores of arms; and in the palace there lived, a virtual prisoner, the last of the old Mogul Emperors, Bahadur Shah—a rallying point for disaffection.

The movement spread like wildfire along the Ganges valley. Jails were broken open, magazines seized, Europeans and Christians, men, women and children, were massacred wholesale; and organised insurgent bands were soon formed. At first the British authorities were slow to take action; but in the North-West the Sikhs stood firm to their alliance with the British; and the Punjab did not rise.

The seizure of Delhi cut the great line of communication which ran across Upper India from Calcutta to Peshawar; though the heroism of a few Englishmen under Lieutenant Willoughby blew up the magazine at Delhi and denied that immense store of ammunition to the rebels. Canning was far away in Eastern Bengal, where there was only a single English regiment, outnumbered ten times by the Sepoys. Westwards, at Benares and Allahabad, there were only native troops—at Cawnpore five Indian regiments and fifty-nine English gunners, with a large non-combatant European population;—at Lucknow three battalions, a regiment and a battery, all natives, with only 570 English infantry. Near Delhi, at Meerut, a powerful British force of all arms was paralysed by a nerveless commander. Only in the Punjab were there sufficient British and loyal native troops to hold their own. Beyond Peshawar stood the wild and uncertain tribes of Afghanistan.

But Canning kept calm. He brought in from other parts of India British troops, and even secured some from Lord Elgin's expedition then on its way to China; while by force and art John Lawrence, a Civil Servant, held the Punjab. Delhi was besieged by the British; Oudh and the North-West Provinces were maintained by the forced marches and incredible exploits of small columns led by Havelock, Outram and Nicholson, and through the courage of the tenuous garrisons in Lucknow and Cawnpore; until a new Commander-in-Chief, Sir Colin Campbell, afterwards Lord Clyde, came at last to their rescue. By the end of the year the fall of Delhi and the final relief of Lucknow brought the war to its real close and the Mutiny was defeated. The old Mogul Emperor was imprisoned for life at Rangoon; his sons had been shot by Hodson of Hodson's Horse. Some smaller centres of resistance remained active for several months; and it was two years before the last rebels were finally beaten.

Meanwhile in England, after the first surprise and shock, a Bill had been introduced in Parliament to transfer the government of India from the East India Company to the Crown. It thus became Lord Canning's lot not only to suppress the Mutiny but to initiate the peaceful revolution that followed it. Through both tasks he preserved his equanimity, being equally abused for his severity and his mercy. After the Bill had been passed he announced it at a Durbar at Allahabad on 1st November 1858, and himself became the first Viceroy. This title was not strictly official but denoted that he personally represented the Sovereign. He and his successors continued to be also Governors-General. In 1859 peace was proclaimed; and Canning followed this up by a progress through the

North of India when he received the homage of the princes. Lord Roberts in "Forty-one Years in India" gives a brilliant first-hand picture of these years.

The Mutiny cost India about £40,000,000 and increased the resulting annual military expenditure by a fourth of that amount. Despite its horrors and expense it was probably of much good both to England and India; for it gave to each a new view of the power of the other and of their own duties if they wished to live in amity and unity. The antiquated and often narrow-minded rule of the East India Company, which had done well enough in its time, now came to an end, and was succeeded by that of the India Office in London where wider and longer political views could be taken.

For a time Canning was unpopular both at home and with the English in India. He was called Clemency Canning because he insisted that culprits should be tried and treated with justice, and that a distinction should be made between instigators of revolt and their ignorant followers; for he had always maintained his courage. He had refused, against the advice of John Lawrence, to retire from the lands beyond the Indus, and by his reliance on the courage of Henry Lawrence Lucknow was held and saved. But the process of pacification was as strenuous and severe as it was criticised.

In 1858 Canning issued a proclamation dealing with the rebel state of Oudh. This document was adversely commented on and the comment published in London by Lord Ellenborough, then President of the Board of Control, an action which greatly annoyed the Queen and the Government; but Canning contented himself with a calm and dignified reply; and Ellenborough eventually had to resign.

Canning's last years in India were devoted to placing the provinces in order, and to confirming the loyalty of chiefs and people, though he still had plenty of opposition even from his own subordinates; and his patience and tenacity were taxed to the utmost. He was laborious at work and not a particularly good man of business.

In 1859 he was advanced to an earldom, and in the following years he held a series of Durbars all over those parts of the country where the worst scenes of the Mutiny had been enacted. He was received with genuine joy and submission, but the journey back to Calcutta in the hot weather impaired his failing health; and he was further shaken by the death of his wife, who died of jungle fever in 1861.

In the following March he retired, and on his arrival in England he was given the Garter. A few weeks later he died in London, on 17th June 1862. He left no issue and all his titles expired. He was buried in Westminster Abbey.

Canning was a man born to success. His father, a man of remarkable talents, had been Prime Minister. He had marked talents himself and was aided by means and connection. At the University, in Parliament and in India he devoted himself to his work with the conscientious character that was his mainstay. Cold, repressed and often opinionated, he was absolutely just; and he carried through the darkest days of a great crisis with the patient and tenacious courage that earned for him the respect of those who best knew what his local circumstances were and what risks he had to run. "Magnanimous, the mirror of honour, he was the pattern of a high-minded and fearless statesman." In Lord Curzon's words, he was calm amid the tumult, silent in the face of obloquy, resolute upon the great and crowning lesson of mercy. He had brave and brilliant men to support him, but it was largely his own guidance and inspiration which brought their work to a successful issue.

G. Richmond pinx.

JAMES BRUCE

8TH EARL OF ELGIN

15

EARL OF ELGIN

1862-1863

JAMES BRUCE, afterwards Earl of Elgin and Kincardine in Scotland, was born in Park Lane, London,
on 20th July 1811, the third but eventually first surviving son of Thomas, 7th and 10th Earl, by Elizabeth,
daughter of James Oswald of Dunnekeir, sometime
Auditor of the Scottish Exchequer. His father, a
lieutenant-general and a representative peer for Scotland,
had had a long and distinguished career as a diplomat,
and whilst Ambassador at Constantinople had secured
from the Parthenon at Athens the famous Elgin marbles,
which he later sold to the British Museum for half what
they had cost him, £74,000. The Bruces were connected
with the old Scottish kings and for five hundred years had
played an honoured part in the history of their country.

James Bruce was educated at Eton and Christ Church,
where he took a first in classics, was President of the Union
and was made a Fellow of Merton. Among his contemporaries were W. E. Gladstone, Dalhousie and Canning,
the two latter of whom were to be his immediate predecessors as Governors-General of India.

In 1840 his elder brother, Lord Bruce, died; and in the
following year he married Elizabeth Mary, daughter of
Charles Cumming Bruce of Dunphail in county Stirling.
He was elected M.P. for Southampton and soon afterwards
seconded the address in Parliament which caused the fall
of Lord Melbourne's Government. Four months later his
father died, and as a Scottish peer he then vacated his
seat in the House of Commons.

Early in 1842 Elgin was appointed Governor of Jamaica.

Here he did really good work in improving the finances, the system of agriculture and the education of the negro population. He left such a satisfactory record that in 1846 he was offered by Lord John Russell the Governor-General-ship of Canada. While in Jamaica Elgin had lost his wife; and he now married Lady Mary Lambton, daughter of the 1st Earl of Durham, who had held the same office a few years earlier. Canada was at that time poor and disunited. The Rebellion of 1838 had not been forgotten; the British and French populations were mutually antag-onistic; and the Free Trade Act of 1846 had cost the millowners heavy losses.

At first Elgin had a difficult time in Canada. He was even stoned when going to open Parliament, and he had to remove the seat of government from Montreal to Quebec and Toronto. But he was cautious, sensible and patient, and by the time his eight years of office were over he had become a popular and successful Governor; among other exploits and mainly by his own personal exertions, he had concluded a valuable reciprocity treaty with the United States. While in Canada he had been made a Knight of the Thistle and given a barony of the United Kingdom with a seat in the House of Lords, and in 1854 when he came home he had a promising reputation.

For two years he remained silent and independent, though Lord Palmerston offered him a place in his Cabinet. Then in 1857 he was asked to go as special Envoy to China in order to settle some long outstanding disputes, if necessary by arms. He was accompanied by a considerable force; but on arriving at Singapore he received despatches from Lord Canning in India informing him of the outbreak of the Mutiny and asking him urgently for help. Elgin could take decisions quickly; he at once sent off the whole of his troops to India; and this undoubtedly bore a great part in finally quelling the rebellion. He went on alone to Hong Kong, but finding his expected reinforcements did not materialise, he sailed back to Calcutta, and even left with Canning the ship of war in which he was travelling.

As soon as fresh troops had arrived he returned to Canton, captured it, and then proceeded to Tientsin, where in 1858 he concluded a satisfactory treaty with the Manchu Emperor, providing for the establishment of a British Legation at Peking, proper facilities for British trade, protection for British subjects and a sufficient war indemnity. He then continued his voyage to Japan, where he made another treaty for the opening of some Japanese ports to British traders. When he got home to England in 1859 he was given the Freedom of the City of London and made a G.C.B.; and soon afterwards he joined Palmerston's Ministry as Postmaster-General.

But the Chinese Government did not ratify the treaty Elgin had made; and he had to be sent out again with a larger contingent of troops than before. After several hazardous adventures of shipwreck near Ceylon (during which he sat calmly on the poop talking to his French colleague) and treacherous assaults by Chinese mandarins, he eventually again defeated their army, destroyed the Emperor's Summer Palace at Peking, and dictated stringent terms of peace under the walls of the capital. His maxim for dealing with the Chinese was "Never make a demand which is not absolutely just, and when you make a just demand see that you get it." He returned to England early in 1861, and a month later was offered the Viceroyalty of India to relieve Lord Canning.

He arrived in Calcutta in March 1862 and found a full and serious programme before him. He was only fifty, but he had recently led a hard life, and he now suffered much from the Indian climate. His chief task was to carry out the many rearrangements resulting from the Mutiny which Canning had left for his completion. After spending some months in Calcutta studying the position, he travelled north to Benares, Agra and Delhi, where he held Durbars and met the local chiefs and officials, to whom his genial manners and social tastes endeared him. He passed the summer at Simla and then started by a mountain journey for Lahore; but in crossing a rocky valley in the Himalayas by a swinging wooden bridge he was put to great physical exertion which brought on a severe heart attack; and a few days later he died, and was buried at Dharmsala on 20th November 1863. Sir Robert Napier and Sir William Denison respectively officiated until the arrival of his successor in the following year. Thirty years later his eldest son became Viceroy of India. The present earl is his grandson.

Elgin was a practical, resolute man with a strong sense of duty and a forceful character. An active and experienced Governor, he liked administration and did it well. Short, stout and florid, with a quick, ready manner, he had plenty of good sense, tact and a love for steady hard work. Anxious to follow the ways of peace, he was forced to have recourse to military measures, but he was a pattern of the best type of public servant, and able to adapt himself to circumstances. Of his fifty-two years of life, eighteen were spent in some of the highest positions under the Crown, always with honour and usually with success.

G. F. Watts pinx.

JOHN LAWRENCE

LORD LAWRENCE

16

LORD LAWRENCE

1863-1869

JOHN LAIRD MAIR LAWRENCE, afterwards 1st Lord Lawrence, was born at Richmond, Yorkshire, on 4th March 1811, the sixth son and eighth child of Lieutenant-Colonel Alexander Lawrence, 19th Foot, by Catherine Letitia, daughter of the Rev. George Knox, Rector of Stabane in Antrim. His father, whose family had been domiciled in Ireland for many years, was a hard-working regular soldier of no fortune or influence, who had won his commission in India, to whose service he sent five of his sons.

John Lawrence was educated at a number of schools as his father's regiment moved from garrison to garrison, but he did not particularly distinguish himself at any of them. History was his principal reading, and at Foyle College in Londonderry he learned of the famous siege of that city. He had always wanted to be a soldier, but being offered a writership in the East India Company's service he sacrificed his own wishes, and after two years' preparation at Haileybury he went out to Calcutta in 1829 with his elder brother Henry and his sister Honoria.

His first post was at Delhi, where he worked as assistant to the Resident and later as Magistrate and Collector in the districts of Panepat and Gurgaon. As a revenue officer he devoted himself to his duties, working morning, noon and night, and acquiring that profound and detailed knowledge of the native customs, agriculture and languages which was later to stand him in such good stead. The provincial government was still patriarchal; and the prosperity of the peasants, on which the whole Indian economy was based, depended on the land tax. This

F   81

Lawrence always assessed low, and in two extensive famines which took place during his early days he acquired a deep sympathy for the humble, hard-worked native population, who soon recognised his goodwill and ability.

After eight years of this solid and useful service he was promoted to be Settlement Officer in Etewah, but being struck down by fever he had to go home on furlough. While in Ireland in August 1842 he married Harriet Catherine, daughter of the Rev. Richard Hamilton, Rector of Culdaff in County Donegal. For some time he then travelled on the Continent to recover his health; but his fever still remained, and he was advised not to return to India. He replied that he must go back there if only to die.

Late in 1842 he was appointed First Civil Judge, Magistrate and Collector in Delhi, where he remained for four years. There in 1845 Lord Hardinge, the Governor-General, met him and was greatly impressed by the "vehement, hard-riding young man." Lawrence's two soldier brothers, Henry and George, had already made themselves known as capable officers; and Hardinge, recognising the future value of this third Lawrence, in 1846 selected him to be Commissioner of the newly acquired Sikh territory. "Send me up John Lawrence" he telegraphed to the Lieutenant-Governor of the North-West Provinces.

The country which Lawrence had to administer lay across the Sutlej and was in an unsettled, discontented and dangerous state; for after the late war many of the Rajahs had been dispossessed, and the stigma of defeat lay heavily on a warlike population. But Lawrence approached his problem in a friendly and statesmanlike spirit, until he gradually acquired the trust and indeed the affection of his new subjects. His brother, now Sir Henry, was Chief Commissioner of the Punjab at Lahore, where John occasionally relieved him; and though the two did not always see eye to eye, they always had the true interests of India at heart. For a time, with C. G. Mansel, these three ruled the Punjab as a Board; and on one occasion, by prompt action, John Lawrence saved the province from a Sikh rebellion. Later on he was himself made Chief Commissioner, and in 1856 he was knighted and given a K.C.B.

When the Mutiny came, it was Lawrence in his civilian capacity who took a large share in its suppression. "Delay," he said, "was only a less misfortune than repulse." He acted as a sort of unofficial Quartermaster-General behind the British troops which were besieging Delhi, supplying them with stores and transport, and also raising considerable levies of regular and irregular troops. His advice to Canning in Calcutta was of the highest and most constant value.

During the Mutiny Lawrence's brother Henry was killed at Lucknow, holding out gallantly to the end against the rebels. John, known all over India as "Jan Larin," a sort of god who could do anything, maintained the loyalty of his own province; and after the Mutiny was over, Lord Canning wrote: "Through him Delhi fell and the Punjab became a source of strength. It is difficult to exaggerate the value of such ability, silence and energy at such a time." After the cessation of hostilities Lawrence was as distinguished as Canning for his clemency.

In 1859 he was again forced to take a rest, so he went back to England for his first real holiday for seventeen years. At home he had become a popular hero. He was created a baronet, sworn a Privy Councillor and given the Freedom of the City of London and a pension of £2000 a year. He was also made a member of the new Council of India. But this London work he soon found too sedentary, and he longed to return to his life in India. The Governorship of Bombay he refused; but at the end of 1863, on Lord Elgin's death, he was offered the Governor-Generalship, and this he accepted, the first Civil Servant since Sir John Shore fifty years earlier to receive it. He had once said to Colin Campbell, "The Governor-Generalship is too good a post for a fellow like me."

His tenure of his new office was not remarkable for many striking events; but he was happy to be again in India. He had to direct his attention to retrenchment and reform more than to expansion and conquest. Finance, sanitation, railways, forestry and irrigation were his interests. Always he maintained his care for the ryot, the backbone of Indian life; while on the frontier his policy was one of vigilant defence. The annexation of Bhutan in 1864 and the Orissa famine in 1866 were the two most salient features of his rule. But he was unsuited both by temperament and training for the post of Viceroy. A man of action, he was intolerant of discussion or departmental files, and he lacked dignity in the conduct of ceremonial.

He remained in India until January 1869, and on finally returning to England he was raised to the peerage as Lord Lawrence. But in Parliament he made little mark, rather concerning himself with beneficent work such as the London School Board, of which he became Chairman, the Church Missionary Society and the management of various hospitals. His eyesight and his health gradually failed, and on 26th July 1879 he died in London at the age of sixty-eight and was buried in Westminster Abbey, a statue being set up to him in Waterloo Place. The present Lord Lawrence is his great-grandson.

Lawrence was a fanatic for duty and work—a rugged token of strength. Pious and severe, with strong military instincts and good military knowledge, he knew his work and the country of his adoption through and through, and he was determined all his life to give of his best and to see justice done. Masterful, impatient of control, unwilling to compromise and with many enemies—neither Dalhousie nor Napier the Commander-in-Chief liked him—he was a heroic, powerful and religious figure who contributed as much as any other Englishman to the survival of English rule in India at the time of its severest test. He well deserved his name of the Saviour of the Punjab.

RICHARD BOURKE

6TH EARL OF MAYO

17

EARL OF MAYO

1869-1872

RICHARD SOUTHWELL BOURKE, first styled Lord Naas and later 6th Earl of Mayo, was born on 21st February 1822 in Dublin, the eldest son of Robert Bourke, afterwards 5th Earl, by Anne Charlotte, only daughter of the Hon. John Jocelyn, fourth son of Robert, 1st Earl of Roden. The Bourkes, formerly de Burghs, were an ancient Irish family established in Mayo and Kildare, who had been raised to the Irish peerage in 1781. Robert Bourke, son of a Bishop of Waterford and grandson of an Archbishop of Dublin, was a strong evangelical; while his wife was equally devoted to religion.

Richard Bourke spent his early years at Hayes in Meath, where he became a good shot and rider. His parents were not well off; so he was educated at home and took his degree at Trinity College, Dublin, without going into residence. At the age of twenty-three he went on a short trip to Russia and wrote a thoughtful and successful book about his travels. Two years later he took an active part in relief work during the Irish famine, when for months he almost lived in the saddle; and in 1847 he was elected M.P. for Kildare, where he had become well known and popular. He then spent some time in London, "a very young man with a fine bearing, one of the best waltzers in town and made much of." In Ireland he was an active sportsman, farmer and horse-breeder.

In Parliament he spoke seldom at first, and only about things he knew. "No discussion," said Lord Derby, "could be so dry but he could enliven it with unforced humour which was one of his greatest characteristics."

In 1848 Bourke married Blanche Wyndham, daughter of the first Lord Leconfield; and a few months later, on the death of his great-uncle, his father succeeded to the Irish earldom; and Richard Bourke then took the courtesy title of Lord Naas.

He was a tall, powerful man, straightforward, active and industrious, a moderate Conservative with a thorough knowledge of his own country; and in 1852 Lord Derby, convinced of his qualifications, appointed him a Privy Councillor and Chief Secretary for Ireland—he was called the Boy Secretary—a post which he filled with much success in the later Tory administrations, sitting first for Coleraine and then for Cockermouth on Lord Leconfield's property in the north of England.

In 1857 he became Master of the Kildare Hounds and within four years had turned its deficit into a balance. In 1867, when his father died, he retained his seat in the House of Commons as well as his office in the Government. His Irish policy was firm in repressing sedition, but generally he was conciliating and moderate, especially as regards religious questions and land compensation. Disraeli, like Derby, had a high opinion of Mayo's sagacity and knowledge of men; and in 1868, just before the fall of his Government, he appointed him Viceroy of India to succeed Lord Lawrence—an appointment which Gladstone on coming into office confirmed; and shortly afterwards, on a vacancy occurring, made him a Knight of St Patrick.

Mayo arrived in India in January 1869, having visited Egypt on his way out. Afghanistan was still to the fore in Indian politics. For six years the country had been torn by civil war; but at last Shir Ali Khan had established himself as Amir; and one of Mayo's first official acts was to assure him of British support and to confirm him as a loyal ally. Although the Amir did not get all he wanted from the Indian Government, a satisfactory agreement was arrived at. Mayo followed a similar friendly policy with other frontier states, and he was particularly wise in peaceful dealings with the great feudatory chiefs, for he disliked punitive expeditions.

Finance always occupied his closest attention. He dealt with deficits by raising the salt and income taxes and reducing expenditure on public works and on the military services. Railway construction he developed by means of loans, and he took charge himself of the Public Works Department as well as that of Foreign Affairs. He had excellent business-like habits.

Agriculture and education were other matters in which he shewed a special interest; the Mayo College at Ajmir was started by him. He travelled about India more than any of his predecessors had done, covering in his three years of rule over 20,000 miles. It was he who really introduced the system of provincial administration that later gave so great an impulse to local government. He worked with tremendous energy, his physical strength and trained mental vigour keeping him in sound health. He had always paid constant and kindly attention to prison discipline and reform; and early in 1872, when visiting the penal settlement in the Andaman Islands in the Bay of Bengal, as he was getting into a boat in the twilight he was stabbed to death, on 8th February, by an embittered Afghan convict, oddly named Shir Ali, who was shortly afterwards executed. This murder, the only one of a British Viceroy or Governor-General in nearly two centuries, caused equal sorrow and resentment in India, England and Ireland. The untimely death of a good ruler when under fifty was deeply regretted.

Mayo's body was embalmed and taken home to Naas, where he was buried two months later. His widow, who survived until 1918, was given an annuity of £1000 by Parliament and a similar amount by the Council of India with a capital sum of £20,000.

Mayo left four sons, one of whom succeeded him in the title; but in the second generation his male issue became extinct; the present earl is a collateral relative.

He was a man of untiring energy, good sense and industry. "He did and said generous things," said Lord Derby, "not because it was politic but because it was his nature." His zeal, courtesy and kindness endeared him to all with whom he came in contact; and the important economic reforms which he introduced in the Indian Government were a valuable and permanent addition to its political system.

His appointment to India had been criticised at first; but his rule was admittedly a success. Queen Victoria called him "able, vigilant and impartial."

W. W. Ouless pinx.

R. Josey s

THOMAS BARING

EARL OF NORTHBROOK

18

EARL OF NORTHBROOK

1872-1876

THOMAS GEORGE BARING, afterwards Lord and Earl of Northbrook, was born in Cumberland Street, London, on 22nd January 1826, the eldest son of Sir Francis Baring, 3rd Baronet, of Stratton Park, Hants, by Jane, daughter of the Hon. Sir George Grey, brother of Earl Grey, the Whig Prime Minister. The Barings, originally a German family, had settled in England early in the eighteenth century and had founded a prosperous banking firm; and for a hundred years they had been distinguished in finance. The grandfather of Thomas had been Chairman of the East India Company; while his father, a Whig M.P., had been Chancellor of the Exchequer under Lord Melbourne and First Lord of the Admiralty under Lord John Russell.

After a private education Thomas Baring went to Christ Church, where he took a second class in classics, and then served as private secretary to several Liberal statesmen. In 1848 he married Elizabeth, daughter of Henry Charles Sturt of Crichel and sister of the 1st Lord Alington. In 1857 he was elected M.P. for Penrhyn and Falmouth; and almost at once Lord Palmerston gave him office as Civil Lord of the Admiralty. Two years later he became Under-Secretary to Sir Charles Wood, Secretary of State for India; and after having filled the same place at the Home Office in 1866 he succeeded his father, who had just been created a peer, as 2nd Lord Northbrook. His wife died in the following year.

For a short time he now occupied himself with his estates in Hampshire, until in Gladstone's Ministry of 1868 he was made Under-Secretary for War; and for three years he was closely concerned with Lord Cardwell's measures for the reorganisation of the Army, being in charge of the Bill in the House of Lords.

At Lord Mayo's death in 1872 Northbrook was selected by Gladstone as Viceroy, a position of which he already had some knowledge from his previous work at the India Office. He was the first Viceroy to enter Calcutta by rail; the approach had hitherto always been made by sea and river. He took as his private secretary his very able cousin Captain Evelyn Baring, afterwards so well known as Lord Cromer, whom Curzon called "perhaps the most famous of all Private Secretaries." Administration and finance were already familiar to Northbrook. Stabilisation was still the principal need in India after the conflicts of the Mutiny and the resulting financial deficits. But he was able to abolish income tax and reduce local expenditure, for he kept a rigid control over public works. In 1874 the great Bengal famine gave him a real chance of shewing his administrative and financial abilities. By well-designed measures, which he initiated and supervised himself, he was able greatly to mitigate its damage. This was really the most successful part of his work in India. His later years were not so happy. He resented the control which Lord Salisbury, now Secretary of State for India, sought to impose on him, often by telegraph; nor did he approve the Home Government's aggressive policy towards Afghanistan. In 1875 he had to supersede the Gaekwar of Baroda for gross misgovernment. In the following year the Prince of Wales, afterwards King Edward VII, paid an official visit to India, a popular and valuable event, and the first of its kind.

A few months later Northbrook resigned his office, and he was then advanced to an earldom. He was only just fifty; but on the death of his uncle Thomas Baring he had inherited a large fortune and a fine collection of pictures, and he now turned with pleasure to his former country pursuits in England. On Gladstone's coming into office in 1880 he resumed his political career, becoming First Lord of the Admiralty with a seat in the Cabinet, where he acted as the Government's principal adviser on Eastern affairs. In this capacity he was largely responsible for the despatch of General Gordon to the Sudan, and in 1884 he went out to advise on Egyptian finance as High Commissioner in Cairo, where his cousin, Evelyn Baring, was now Consul-General. Northbrook's actions at this juncture were not universally approved; and it was also suggested that he had been too thrifty about the Navy.

Latterly he did not see eye to eye with his colleagues in the Liberal Party, and on the Home Rule question coming to the fore he gradually moved towards the Unionists, though he refused office from both Gladstone and Salisbury. His interests turned more and more to the country, where he took a prominent part in local affairs; and in 1889 he was made Lord-Lieutenant of Hampshire. Fifteen years later, on 15th November 1904, he died at Stratton and was buried at Micheldever. His eldest and only surviving son left no male issue; and on his death in 1929 the earldom became extinct. The present peer is his great-nephew.

Northbrook was a Whig of the best tradition, a thoroughly competent administrator with a rapid mastery of complicated financial problems. In India he was determined to govern for the benefit of the native population, an aim in which he succeeded. A Fellow of the Royal Society, with a wide knowledge of art, he belonged to an exceptionally gifted family, four members of which within the space of fifty-seven years had received peerages. A man of high character, sound judgment, industrious and impartial, Northbrook was never a great speaker or politician; he was a quiet, dignified and reserved country gentleman who followed the old Whig tradition of capable service to his country.

G. F. Watts pinx.

EDWARD ROBERT BULWER-LYTTON

EARL OF LYTTON

19

EARL OF LYTTON

1876-1880

EDWARD ROBERT BULWER LYTTON, afterwards
Lord and Earl of Lytton, was born in Hertford Street,
Mayfair, on 8th November 1831, the only son of Edward
Bulwer, 1st Lord Lytton, by Rosina, daughter of Francis
Wheeler of Lizzard Cornell, County Limerick. His family,
which had changed its name several times by marriage,
inherited the Knebworth estate in Hertfordshire from the
Robinsons in 1834; and his father, Edward Bulwer, a distinguished novelist and politician, was made a baronet in
1838 and a peer in 1866, after being Secretary of State for
the Colonies.

Lytton, who had shewn remarkable literary talents as
a boy, was educated at Harrow and at Bonn in Germany,
where he devoted himself to languages. At the age of
nineteen he went to Washington and later to Florence as
private secretary to his uncle, Sir Henry Bulwer, afterwards Lord Dalling, the British Minister. There he was
a friend of the Brownings. He was then appointed a paid
attaché in the Diplomatic Service, and served in succession
at a number of European posts, including St Petersburg
and Vienna. Lord Redesdale, speaking of the younger
members of the Foreign Service in those days, said that
two were *facile principes*, Julian Fane and Robert Lytton.
"Those two we neophytes worshipped as demigods."

Like his father, Lytton was a clever writer. Before he
was thirty he had published, under the name of Owen
Meredith, two volumes of poems which made a considerable
impression in London, where he became a friend of Charles
Dickens and other literary lights. Nor were his talents

confined to verse, for while in Austria he wrote some valuable commercial reports for the Foreign Office.

In 1869, while Secretary of Legation at Lisbon, he married Edith, daughter of the Hon. Edward Villiers, a brother of Lord Clarendon the Foreign Minister. She it was who kept him to his public career, for his own predilections were for poetry. In later years he published *Lucile* and other poems copied to some extent from Browning, Tennyson and George Sand, but shewing evidence of much ability. His father was said to have envied their success.

In 1872 he was promoted to be Minister in Lisbon, and in the following year he succeeded his father as a peer. In 1875 he refused the Governorship of Madras. A year later he was made Viceroy of India—Disraeli's tribute to literary merit; he called Lytton "a man of ambition, imagination, vanity and strength." It was Lady Lytton who pressed her husband to accept the post.

When Lytton arrived in India the scene appeared tranquil. But after a gorgeous Durbar at Delhi to proclaim Queen Victoria as Empress of India he had to deal with a widespread and devastating famine in the South. He raised large funds and set up an effective relief organisation to meet such calamities in the future—a system that was permanently maintained.

In 1877 fresh trouble began in Afghanistan. Lytton and the Home Government favoured a forward policy and were determined to have British representatives near the Russian frontiers in Central Asia; but to this the Amir, Shir Ali, would not agree, though he received a Russian agent at Kabul. Lytton refused to tolerate this discrimination, and in 1879 sent into the country a triple expedition which dethroned the Amir and installed his son in his place. But shortly afterwards the British envoy in Kabul was murdered by Afghans. Lytton acted promptly, and at the shortest notice despatched a force under Sir Frederick (later Lord) Roberts which took Kabul and set up Abdur-rahman, a cousin of Shir Ali, as the new Amir.

At this moment the Conservative Government in England was defeated: and Lytton resigned with it. The expenses of the Afghan War were found to be much greater than had been expected; and further errors were also discovered when the Indian budget was audited. Lytton's general policy, however, though including some restrictions on the Press, much criticised by the Liberals at the time, was afterwards approved. His despatches were models of literary style. With an engaging disregard of established etiquette, he used to write to Queen Victoria in the first person. "Her Majesty," according to Curzon, "was enchanted with their unconventional and interesting character."

For some years Lytton now took no active part in public affairs, until in 1887 he was appointed Ambassador in Paris. For this post, which he hesitated about taking, for he still wished to retire and write, he was eminently suited by his knowledge of the French, their language and literature. He filled the Embassy with poets and painters and made it a rather Bohemian *Salon des Arts*. During his residence in Paris he published the *Ring of Amasis*, not one of his most successful efforts: as an old man he wrote less easily. In Paris he was a most popular British representative: "beloved as no English Ambassador had been since Waterloo." During his mission the visits of the Prince of Wales started the ideas of the Entente. Lytton died there of heart failure on 24th November 1891, and was given a State funeral.

Thirty-four years later his elder son, when Governor of Bengal, acted as Viceroy for some months while Lord Reading was on leave in England. The present (3rd) earl is his younger son.

Lytton was a man of high literary ability, a scholar, a diplomat and a competent ruler, but a poet first and foremost. He had foibles, sometimes disregarded convention and was capricious; but he had perfect discretion; his ideas of government were generous and sound; and his Indian measures are now generally regarded as statesmanlike and wise.

G. F. Watts pinx.

GEORGE FREDERICK ROBINSON

MARQUESS OF RIPON

20

MARQUESS OF RIPON

1880-1884

GEORGE FREDERICK SAMUEL ROBINSON, after-wards Earl and Marquess of Ripon, was born on 24th October 1827, at 10 Downing Street, the second but only surviving son of Frederick ("Prosperity") Robinson, who as Viscount Goderich was one of the most ineffective of British Prime Ministers for a few months in the year of his son's birth, and was created Earl of Ripon six years later. His mother was Lady Sarah Hobart, daughter of the 4th Earl of Buckinghamshire. The Robinsons were a wealthy Yorkshire family who for more than a century by sufficient talent, useful alliances and assiduous public service in politics and diplomacy had acquired a position in the Whig Party that could not be ignored.

As a boy George Robinson, who was styled Lord Goderich, was educated privately, going neither to a public school nor to a university. In 1849 he was attached for a short time to a special mission to Brussels under Sir Henry Ellis for negotiating peace between Austria and Piedmont; and soon after his return to London he married his cousin Henrietta Anne Theodosia, daughter of Henry Vyner of Cautley. He was early interested in the Christian Socialist movement, was a friend of Charles Kingsley and Thomas Hughes, and wrote a democratic pamphlet which was held by his mentors to be too radical for publication.

In 1852 he was elected Liberal member for Hull but was unseated on petition for "treating." Next year he was returned for Huddersfield in support of Palmerston, and later he sat for Cobden's former seat in West Yorkshire. In January 1859 he succeeded his father as Earl of Ripon, and in the following November he also succeeded his uncle as Earl de Grey, a senior title. In this year he was made Under-Secretary for War, and took an active part in the Volunteer movement; and he afterwards held the same position in the India Office. Returning to the War Office in 1863, he succeeded Sir George Cornewall Lewis as Secretary of State, being then sworn a Privy Councillor; and in Russell's government he went to the India Office in a similar capacity.

When Gladstone formed his ministry in 1868 de Grey was made Lord President of the Council and given the Garter. Though only forty, he was now one of the recognised leaders of the Liberal Party, being rich, influential and industrious. In 1871 he acted as Chairman of the High Commission for the settlement of American claims in respect of the privateering of the s.s. *Alabama*. This he did well; and in June he was raised to a marquessate as Marquess of Ripon.

In August 1873 he resigned his political office and next month became a Roman Catholic; and thenceforward he was regarded as one of the leaders of that religion in this country. For several years he now remained in political retirement, until on Gladstone's return to office in 1880 he was appointed Viceroy of India. Blunt says that it had been intended by the Cabinet that he should break up the ring of permanent officials who ruled in Simla; but Ripon was not a man of iron, and did not do so.

In Calcutta Ripon found himself confronted with the Afghan question, and he at once took a strong line. He had Abdurrahman Khan proclaimed Amir on the condition that he had no relations with Russia; and after the British defeat in Maiwand he let Sir Frederick Roberts march from Kabul to Kandahar, which was brought under the Amir's rule. Ripon's military policy was thus triumphant in his first year in India. In domestic affairs he was less fortunate. He repealed Lytton's restrictions on the Press and made efforts to encourage native responsibility and self-government in small areas. He also did his best to place Englishmen under the same criminal law as Indians, even when administered by native judges. But for these changes the European community was not yet ready, nor was the country sufficiently educated in Western ideas. This measure, the "Ilbert Bill," was so unpopular that several tea-planters in Assam proposed to kidnap the Viceroy on his way to a shoot. His son went instead; but Ripon's advanced policy had to be modified. Otherwise he was a wise administrator, closely interested in the people's welfare. His work for education and economy was enduring and sound, and he definitely brought the Liberal idea into Indian politics.

He returned to England in December 1884, and in Gladstone's ministry (to whom Granville described him as "a persistent man with wealth") he served as First Lord of the Admiralty and later as Secretary of State for the Colonies. A convinced supporter of Home Rule for Ireland, he received the Freedom of the city of Dublin, and there was some talk of making him Lord-Lieutenant of Ireland, to which his religion was a bar. To get over this a "Ripon and Russell Relief Bill" was canvassed (Sir Charles Russell, also a Roman Catholic, was an aspirant for the Woolsack); but it came to nothing.

When after ten years in Opposition Campbell-Bannerman came into office in 1905, Ripon as Lord Privy Seal became leader of the House of Lords. He was seventy-eight, and in a difficult position with a large majority against him, but he acquitted himself with tact, good humour and courage, speaking little and shortly; "but his words full of sense and knowledge." On Asquith's becoming Premier in 1908 Ripon finally resigned; and a year later he died at Studley Royal, on 9th July 1909. He was succeeded by his only son, on whose death without a male heir all his titles became extinct.

Ripon was a trained statesman with a good tradition behind him, a loyal colleague, an experienced administrator and a convinced and religious Radical; throughout his long and active life he never deviated from a high code of honour and duty, though he was not of any outstanding brilliancy or capacity.

G. F. Watts pinx.

FREDERICK HAMILTON-TEMPLE-BLACKWOOD

MARQUESS OF DUFFERIN AND AVA

21

MARQUESS OF DUFFERIN
1884-1888

FREDERICK TEMPLE BLACKWOOD, later
Hamilton-Temple-Blackwood, afterwards Earl and
Marquess of Dufferin, was born on 21st June 1826, in the
Via Maggio, Florence, the only son of Price Blackwood,
4th Lord Dufferin and Clandeboye in the peerage of
Ireland, by Helen Selina, eldest daughter of Thomas
Sheridan. His mother was the best-looking and most
accomplished of three famous sisters, the other two being
Mrs Caroline Norton and the Duchess of Somerset of the
Eglinton Tournament,—Wilfrid Blunt called her the most
delightful of women. His father, a captain in the Navy,
and a thorough sailor, "frank, open and kind," died when
Blackwood was just fifteen and still at Eton; and his
mother was the formative influence of his early years.
The young Irishman went on to Christ Church, where
he was President of the Oxford Union, and he afterwards travelled for a time in the Near East. In Ireland
he managed his estates, and in the social world in London
he made many friends. As he was a promising Liberal,
Lord John Russell in 1849 appointed him a Lord in Waiting,
though Queen Victoria thought him "too good-looking"
for that post.

Dufferin was accordingly given a peerage of the United
Kingdom, and in the House of Lords he spoke forcibly
and well. A keen and fearless yachtsman, he was up
in the Baltic during the Crimean War, and at the siege
of Bomarsund he shewed his courage in the trenches. He
afterwards wrote an arresting account of his voyage to
Iceland and Spitsbergen in *Letters from High Latitudes.*

In 1860 he accompanied Sir Henry Bulwer as Special Commissioner in Asiatic Turkey to enquire into the massacres of Christians there and in Syria; and his proposal to appoint an independent Governor of the Lebanon was adopted. For these services he was made a Knight of the Bath and subsequently of St Patrick.

In 1862, on his marriage to Harriet, daughter of Archibald Rowan Hamilton of Killyleah Castle in County Down, he added the latter name to his own; and his rapid career of success now began.

In 1864 he entered Palmerston's ministry as Under-Secretary for India; in 1868 Gladstone made him Chancellor of the Duchy of Lancaster and Paymaster-General. Three years later he was raised to an earldom and in 1872 appointed Governor-General of Canada. In Canada he found plenty to do in quelling the sequels of the Red River Rebellion and in calming the storms resulting from the various plans for building the transcontinental railway. In both he was successful.

During his term of office the Supreme Court of Canada was set up; and a ballot system of voting was introduced for the Canadian House of Commons. A recent history written by a Canadian speaks of him as one of their ablest Governors-General. When he left the Dominion in 1878 it was "loyal and united."

He was sent almost at once by Beaconsfield as Ambassador to St Petersburg, and two years later was transferred to Constantinople, where he had to superintend the introduction of reforms in Armenia.

The revolt of Arabi Pasha in Egypt involved Dufferin in complicated diplomatic negotiations with the Sultan of Turkey; but his tact and patience enabled him to carry them through satisfactorily, and for a time he became the central figure of the European Powers in the Near East.

After the defeat of Arabi at Tel-el-Kebir Dufferin was sent to Cairo to reorganise the Egyptian administration.

His efforts towards setting up a representative government did not succeed, but they were recognised by his promotion to a G.C.B.; and in December 1884, on the retirement of Lord Ripon from India, the post of Viceroy was offered him.

His qualities and knowledge were well suited to the solution of the problems then occupying India—land, a free Press and local government. Dufferin's natural disposition and political sympathies inclined him to reform, while his conciliatory manners and friendly speeches helped him to get his measures adopted. Despite his literary gifts he was not a great writer of minutes or despatches: he left much to his private secretary, Sir D. Mackenzie Wallace, afterwards Foreign Editor of *The Times*, "who could even reproduce his signature with lifelike fidelity." At a Durbar in Rawalpindi in 1885 Dufferin entertained the Amir of Afghanistan, who was greatly pleased by his reception. The dangerous Penjdeh incident on the Russo-Afghan border was surmounted, and the principle of a railway extension in Baluchistan was conceded. It was in this year that the first Indian National Congress met.

Dufferin now found it necessary to declare war on King Thebaw of Ava in Burma, whose tyranny over his own subjects had been followed by persistent maltreatment of British residents. After a short campaign the independent part of Burma and the Shan States were annexed; and the Viceroy then visited the country and officially inaugurated British rule. Two later expeditions in Sikkim and on the North-West Frontier did equally well.

During these years Lady Dufferin's beneficent work for supplying medical services to the women of India had made her name deservedly popular; and when Dufferin gave up his post in 1888 he was loaded with honours, being made a marquess as Lord Dufferin and Ava and appointed Lord Warden of the Cinque Ports. He was presented with the freedom of several English cities, and received honorary degrees from Oxford, Cambridge, Dublin and Harvard Universities.

Almost at once he was sent as British Ambassador to Rome, and two years later to Paris. One of the present writer's distant but enduring recollections is seeing him and Lady Dufferin receiving their guests at the head of the Embassy stairs in Paris: he looked the ideal ambassador, distinguished, cryptic and urbane. He retired finally from the public service at the age of seventy in 1897. He was not well off financially, and he then inadvisedly accepted the chairmanship of a mining venture which issued fraudulent accounts, failed and ruined many investors—the Whitaker Wright scandal. Dufferin pluckily faced the shareholders—for though he was ignorant of the actions of his subordinates he was none the less responsible for them. This calamity and the death in 1900 of his eldest son Lord Ava at Ladysmith in the South African War clouded the close of his life. He died at his house at Clandeboye near Belfast on 12th February 1902. Two of his younger sons were subsequently killed; as was his grandson, the 4th marquess, outside the walls of Ava, from which his title came, in 1945. The present marquess is his great-grandson.

Handsome, talented, able and popular, Dufferin started with everything before him; and his long career in some of the highest posts under the Crown met with equal success and recognition. He was seldom idle, and quite late in life he started to learn Persian. His courtesy and appearance were those of the ideal diplomat. There is an excellent caricature of him drawn by his son, Lord Basil Blackwood, in Belloc's *The Modern Traveller*.

Philip de Laszlo pinx.

HENRY CHARLES PETTY-FITZMAURICE

5TH MARQUESS OF LANSDOWNE

22

MARQUESS OF LANSDOWNE

1888-1894

HENRY CHARLES KEITH PETTY-FITZMAURICE, afterwards 5th Marquess of Lansdowne, was born on 14th January 1845, the eldest son of Henry, 4th Marquess, by his second wife, the Hon. Emily Jane Mercer-Nairne, daughter of Auguste, Count de Flahaut, by Margaret, daughter of Admiral Lord Keith and Baroness Nairne in her own right. The Fitzmaurices were a very ancient Irish family who had inherited large landed estates in Kerry and had increased them by marriage with the heiress of Sir William Petty in the eighteenth century. Their principal home was at Bowood in Wiltshire, and among their ancestors they reckoned Lord Shelburne, the Whig Prime Minister, 1782-83, and Lord Henry Petty, Chancellor of the Exchequer in 1806-7, who refused a dukedom fifty years later. He, the 4th Marquess, had been for many years Chairman of the Great Western Railway; and his wife's father, a reputed son of Talleyrand, was sometime French Ambassador in England.

By blood and tradition Lord Clanmaurice, as he was first called, was thus destined for a diplomatic and parliamentary career. He was educated at Eton, where Arthur Balfour was his fag, and at Balliol, but he never had the chance of sitting in the House of Commons, for at the age of twenty-one he succeeded his father and took his seat in the House of Lords. Almost at once he was made a Junior Whip, and in November 1869 he married Lady Maud Hamilton, youngest daughter of the 1st Duke of Abercorn. From 1872 to 1874 he was Under-Secretary for War; and when the Liberal Government returned to office in 1880 he went for a few months in the same capacity to the India Office. He did not, however, agree with Gladstone's Irish policy, and having resigned his political office opposed him in Parliament. In the meanwhile he paid close attention to his Irish estates, developing, housing, replanting and remitting rents.

In 1883 Lansdowne was appointed Governor-General of Canada, where he remained for five years. In 1885 he had to deal with a small but dangerous rebellion in the North-West Territory led by Louis Riel, a French-Canadian half-breed who had been concerned in the Red River Rebellion fifteen years earlier; but this was quickly quelled. Lansdowne's Military Secretary, Lord Melgund, a regular officer in the Scots Guards, acted as Chief of Staff to the Expedition; he was afterwards himself to be Governor-General as Lord Minto.

Lansdowne's later years in Canada were quiet and successful, being mainly signalised by the final completion of the Canadian-Pacific Railway and an amicable settlement with the United States of the long-standing question of the New-foundland Fisheries.

On returning to England he remained opposed to Home Rule; and Lord Salisbury offered him a place in the Conservative Government. This Lansdowne refused, but in the following year he accepted the post of Viceroy of India. Here again he had a comparatively peaceful term of office, except for a short rising in the mountain state of Manipur. His policy was cautious; and he never allowed dangerous questions to become acute, strengthening the Army and the frontiers. He had an admirable private secretary in Sir John Ardagh, afterwards Director of Military Intelligence in London.

In 1893 Lansdowne made a settlement with Afghanistan; and he afterwards dealt successfully with the thorny question of regulating the Indian currency after the fall of the rupee. The retention of the opium traffic under State control was another important matter that he satisfactorily composed. It was under Lansdowne that the system of Imperial contingents of troops maintained by the Indian princes was inaugurated, and the legislative and local provincial councils in native centres developed— the earliest active inception of Indian self-government. His wide hospitality and agreeable bearing made him and his wife very popular; and when in 1894 he returned to England he was given the Garter, the only recommendation to that order made by Lord Rosebery.

Lansdowne subsequently declined the Embassy at St Petersburg; but when Lord Salisbury became Premier in 1895 he joined his Cabinet as a Liberal-Unionist as Secretary of State for War. Here he had the delicate task of replacing the old Duke of Cambridge as Commander-in-Chief by Lord Wolseley, and of reorganising the somewhat antiquated system in the War Office.

During the earlier part of the South African War Lansdowne came in for much public criticism, but he stood loyally by his military advisers and made no attempt to shift the blame for lack of preparation on to their shoulders. In 1900 he was made Foreign Secretary, a post for which he was eminently suited. He had a thorough knowledge and experience of world affairs; he spoke French perfectly and he had a large circle of friends on the Continent. His principal work at the Foreign Office was the Japanese Alliance in 1902 and the Anglo-French Entente of 1904, towards which King Edward VII did much to help.

In 1903 Salisbury died and Lansdowne became the Conservative leader in the House of Lords. Under the ensuing Liberal Government it fell to him to attempt some arrangement when various Liberal Bills were thrown out in the Lords; and eventually it was he who secured the passage of the Parliament Bill in 1911. In these negotiations and in those with Ireland he was always the peacemaker.

In the First World War he joined the Coalition Government as Minister without Portfolio. The loss of his second son early in the war had greatly depressed him; and in 1916 he made a proposal to the Cabinet for a compromise peace which perhaps was partly responsible for the fall of the Asquith Ministry. Not being a member of the new Government under Lloyd George, Lansdowne later felt free to make his proposals public. His view was that a victory after total exhaustion would hardly be worth winning. But his letter to the *Daily Telegraph* was generally repudiated, both by the Government and the Press; and he was widely attacked for it.

In 1918 when the war came to an end he retired to the country, and in 1922 had the sorrow of having his favourite Irish home, Derreen in County Kerry, looted and destroyed by Irish Irregulars. Some years later, on 3rd June 1927, he died suddenly at his younger daughter's home, Newtown Anner, in Tipperary, and was buried at Bowood. He left several children; the present marquess is his grandson.

Lansdowne was a modest, cultivated, able but retiring man, a great county magnate, never anxious for office, but feeling it his duty to fulfil the responsibilities of his position. As a young man he was a good rider, shot and angler. He was also a sound scholar, a well-read historian, an able speaker and debater and a capable administrator. He was always a hard worker and used to write standing up at a high desk at Bowood. He knew much about many things, art, agriculture, botany, sport and the colonies among them—and he had a wide range of sympathies with his many British, Indian and foreign friends. An honest, well-schooled and successful statesman, he left both Canada and India contented and peaceful, and at home he rendered valuable services to his own country, as his predecessors had done in the past. A patrician by descent, wealth, education and tradition, he was regarded in India as the highest type of a real sahib. The American Ambassador, Walter Page, called him the most complete aristocrat he had ever met.

Sir George Reid pinx.

VICTOR ALEXANDER BRUCE

9TH EARL OF ELGIN

23

EARL OF ELGIN

1894-1899

VICTOR ALEXANDER BRUCE, afterwards 9th Earl of Elgin, and 13th of Kincardine, was born at Montreal in Canada on 16th May 1849, the eldest son of James Bruce, the 8th Earl, by his second wife, Lady Mary Louisa Lambton, daughter of the 1st Earl of Durham. At the time of his birth his father was Governor-General of Canada, as his maternal grandfather had been previously. He was educated at Glenalmond and at Eton, and while there in 1863 he succeeded his father, who had died in India after a short term as Viceroy.

Elgin went on to Balliol, where he took a second class both in Mods and Greats, and then, settling down as a country landlord in Fife, began to interest himself in Liberal politics, becoming Chairman of the Scottish Liberal Association. In 1876 he married Lady Constance Mary Carnegie, daughter of the 9th Earl of Southesk. As a Home Ruler he was given office in Gladstone's short Government of 1886, first as Treasurer of the Household and then as First Commissioner of Works, being also sworn of the Privy Council and made Lord-Lieutenant of Fife.

After the Liberals came back to power in 1892, Elgin was offered and accepted the post of Viceroy of India, which, it was understood, had been refused by Sir Henry Norman, a distinguished soldier. He arrived in Bombay early in 1894 at the beginning of a Reform agitation. Native intellectual opinion was now questioning the subservience of India to British policy. The rupee had again fallen in value; and to balance the exchange import duties were imposed—an unpopular measure. Elgin's order that official members of the Legislative Council must vote as they were told to do was hotly resented; and a number of troubles on the North-West Frontier—in Chitral, Malakand and Waziristan—involved several difficult and expensive military expeditions. In 1895 the separate control by the Governors of the troops in Bombay, Madras and Bengal was abolished and all were placed under the Commander-in-Chief in India.

In 1896 bubonic plague began, followed by the greatest famine ever yet known in India. It affected seventy million people and lasted for several years. These misfortunes darkened much of Elgin's tenure of office. In 1897 the North-West border tribes rose again; and the Tirah expedition resulted. Lord Rosebery, speaking of Elgin during this time, praised his patient calmness in confronting his difficulties.

Elgin was not a Lawrence, but a careful, sensible and industrious man with no particular advantages of appearance or manner, rather shy, reserved and silent, and perhaps not always doing his undoubted talents sufficient justice. His Liberal politics also made it harder for him to withstand agitation. But his services satisfied the Government, for when he came back to England in 1899 he was made a Knight of the Garter by Salisbury, the Conservative Prime Minister; and he then became successively Chairman of two important Royal Commissions, one to enquire into the expenditure in the South African War and another as to the union of the non-established Churches in Scotland. Both of these he managed with real success.

In 1905, in Campbell-Bannerman's Liberal Ministry, Elgin was made Colonial Secretary, Mr Winston Churchill being his Under-Secretary; and in that position he was largely concerned in setting up the Union of South Africa; but to Indian constitutional development he was much less attracted, nor was he in sympathy with the left wing of the Radical Government, particularly as regards its attitude to Chinese labour in South Africa. He said that he declined to be a mere partisan. Perhaps for these reasons he was not included in Asquith's Cabinet of 1908, though he is believed to have been offered a marquessate, which he declined.

His wife had died in 1910; and three years later he married Gertrude Lilian, daughter of Captain William Sherbrook, R.N., of Oxton Hall, Nottinghamshire, and widow of Captain F. C. A. Ogilvy, R.N. In 1914 he became Chancellor of Aberdeen University, and he was also Chairman of the Carnegie Trust. He died at Bromhall on 18th January 1917 at the age of sixty-eight. The present earl is his eldest son.

Elgin had many of the qualities of his father. He was patient, careful, judicial, able and conscientious. The two Elgins are the only example of father and son who held the great office of Viceroy of India. Like his colleagues in the Government, Aberdeen, Campbell-Bannerman, Munro-Ferguson and Rosebery, Elgin was a sound and sober Scot and a Victorian Liberal, though, like many of that political faith, he stuck to his own particular standards and would not always toe the party line. He wore a beard, disliked uniform and was no great hand at ceremonial. His lot in India fell in evil times; but he had a fine tradition of public service which he thoroughly fulfilled with modest and honest distinction.

111

J. S. Sargent pinx.   John Cooke s

GEORGE NATHANIEL CURZON

MARQUESS CURZON OF KEDLESTON

24

MARQUESS CURZON

1899-1904 and 1904-1905

GEORGE NATHANIEL CURZON, afterwards Earl
and Marquess Curzon, was born at Kedleston Hall,
Derbyshire, on 11th January 1859, the eldest son of the
Rev. Alfred Curzon, 4th Baron Scarsdale and Rector of
Kedleston, by Blanche, daughter of Joseph Senhouse of
Netherhall, Cumberland.

The Curzons were an ancient family dating back to
the Crusades and living in a magnificent country mansion
and park; and George Curzon inherited all the pride and
traditions of his ancestors. After a hard early upbringing
under a tyrannical governess he went to Eton, where every
success greeted him. He became Captain of the Oppidans,
a member of Pop where he spoke on India, and was
sent up for good twenty-three times. Under the tutor-
ship of Oscar Browning he travelled in Europe, and
from Sir James Stephen he acquired an early interest in
the East. Speaking, reading, writing and collecting
absorbed him. At the age of nineteen a curvature of the
spine first attacked him, the pain of which followed him
through life. To resist it he worked like a fanatic. At
Balliol he became friendly with the future Lords Salisbury,
Selborne and Midleton; he took a 1st in Mods and was
elected President of the Union; but in Greats he only
took a 2nd. In 1886, however, he was elected a Fellow
of All Souls.

On leaving Oxford he travelled in the Near East with
Edward Lyttelton, afterwards Headmaster of Eton. His
speeches had already gained him a political and literary
reputation; and he entered London society with *éclat* and

H   113

soon became one of the leading figures in the eclectic Crabbet Club, and among the so-called "Souls."

To supplement his limited income he wrote for the Press and served as private secretary to Lord Salisbury; and after a first defeat for South Derbyshire he was elected as a Conservative M.P. for Southport in 1886.

Most of the next two years he spent in Persia, India, Central Asia, the Pamirs, the Far East and the United States. He travelled hard and wrote reviews for newspapers while on these journeys, afterwards producing several excellent and well-informed books, some of which are still regarded as classics.

On his journeys Curzon had learnt much about the frontiers of India and had made the acquaintance of many leading personalities of the Indian and neighbouring states, and in 1891 he was appointed Under-Secretary at the India Office. When the Tory Government went out of office in 1892 he set off to Afghanistan and there met the powerful and mysterious Amir Abdurrahman Khan.

In April 1895 he married Mary Leiter, a beautiful and wealthy daughter of Levi Leiter, an American millionaire. In the same year he was made Under-Secretary for Foreign Affairs under Lord Salisbury the Prime Minister, who was himself also Foreign Secretary. Curzon was now sworn a Privy Councillor, and by his remarkable knowledge and ready debating power became an important figure in the House of Commons—when some distant place was mentioned he had always "been there" and knew it personally. He was not always an easy or docile lieutenant to his chief nor a popular colleague, but his talents, industry and information were indisputable.

In August 1898 he was offered and accepted the Viceroyalty of India, being then created an Irish baron so that he might retain the right of sitting in the House of Commons. On 3rd January 1899 he was installed in Calcutta. Not yet forty years of age, he had already arrived at the zenith of his life and ambition; though he is believed to have once said that he regarded the Gold Medal of the Royal Geographical Society as his greatest honour. He secured as his private secretary an able and much loved former Indian Civil Servant, Sir Walter Lawrence.

Curzon took his own line at once, going straight to the root of things, setting aside the traditional routine of departmental procedure and working day and night. This gave him a great name but did not make him much liked by his local subordinates or by the authorities at home. He imposed his will on the sheikhs in the Persian Gulf; he put on duties to protect the Indian sugar industry; he made a treaty with Tibet, and he tried to reduce the status of the Madras and Bombay Presidencies. He formed a new North-Western Province, divided Bengal into two portions and settled with the Nizam of Hyderabad the disputed question of the status of Berar. In 1903 a magnificent Durbar to celebrate the accession of King Edward VII gave Curzon the opportunity of shewing his talent for splendour and ceremonial at which he excelled, managing every detail himself.

He spoke his mind and had few illusions. He once advised the present writer to read much about a country before travelling in it (Bacon's view); and on another occasion he stressed the constant wish of Russia to get to India, and the ignorance of British merchants about the possibilities of trade with China.

In India his policy was to make the country "a homogeneous compound instead of a heterogeneous mixture," and this he believed could only be attained by a strong central government that controlled both princes and provinces. He abolished internal differences of rule and promoted uniformity in education and fiscal systems.

In the meantime Lord Kitchener had arrived in India as Commander-in-Chief, and disputes soon arose between him and the Viceroy. The existing system in the Army was that of a dual control—an independent military member as well as the Commander-in-Chief sat on the Viceroy's Council. But Kitchener wished to be alone and supreme in the Army. While this quarrel was simmering Curzon went home on leave in 1904, his term of office having been extended to seven years. He had recently been made Lord Warden of the Cinque Ports; and at Walmer Castle Lady Curzon fell ill.

At the end of 1904 he returned to India, leaving his wife in England; Lord Ampthill had been in charge during his absence. Curzon again threw all his energies into fresh work, paying special attention to the preservation of the Indian historical monuments, irrigation, finance and the increasing suggestions of devolution of government. But the struggle with Kitchener went on; and only after the latter had threatened to resign was a compromise arrived at. A new military member of Council was then appointed, unfortunately without Curzon's approval; so he himself resigned—returning to England at the end of 1905 embittered and, as he thought, ill-treated. He was not on the best of terms with St John Brodrick, the Secretary of State for India, or with Arthur Balfour, the Prime Minister, who both thought his methods too autocratic.

Six months later Lady Curzon died; and for a time Curzon now kept away from political affairs, though he was elected a representative peer for Ireland, which gave him a seat in the House of Lords.

He now took up many other interests—the Royal Geographical Society, of which he became President; the National Gallery, of which he was a Trustee; universal military service; the restoration of ancient buildings; and particularly the needs of Oxford University, of which he was elected Chancellor in 1907. In 1911 he was promoted to an earldom, with a barony in remainder to his daughters—for he had no sons.

When the war of 1914 came Curzon resumed office as Lord Privy Seal in the Coalition Ministry of 1915, and in the following year he received the Garter and joined the Inner Cabinet in Lloyd George's Government. In this year he succeeded his father as 5th Lord Scarsdale.

In January 1917 he married Grace, widow of Alfred Duggan and daughter of J. M. Hinds, formerly United States Minister in Brazil. He became Lord President of the Council and Leader of the House of Lords, and he then began to entertain again both in Carlton House Terrace in London and in the country, where he bought or rented several large places as well as Kedleston. In politics he was against a Jewish state in Palestine or Parliamentary government in India—which he had formerly favoured. He recognised the agelong aristocratic principle among the Indian peoples and had no great sympathy with the *Vakil Raj* or Lawyer Rule of Congress. He agreed, however, to support a Home Rule policy in Ireland rather against his own wishes; and he also changed his views about Women's Suffrage and did not oppose it in Parliament.

After the war and during the Paris Peace Conference he acted first as temporary and later as actual Foreign Minister. But he was never in complete control; for Lloyd George, the Prime Minister, kept the reins of the Foreign Office in his own hands. In Persia Curzon's policy was not successful; his advice on Egypt and in the Turco-Greek dispute was not taken; so he had the unpleasant rôle of bearing the blame for the errors of others—indeed he was not always consulted. In June 1921, perhaps as a compensation, he was created a marquess—he had a great respect for rank. The rifts in the Coalition Government were now broadening; Curzon could not tolerate his position; and he was probably not sorry when in November 1922 a new Ministry was formed under Bonar Law.

As Foreign Secretary Curzon went out to represent the British Government at the Lausanne Conference, and by his knowledge and manner completely dominated it, being firmer than he had ever been before. In May 1923 Bonar Law resigned owing to ill-health. Curzon had with some reason expected the succession, for he had been in politics for thirty years, had held many high offices, and was the most talented and able of the Conservatives; but Stanley Baldwin was chosen in his place. This blow was probably the bitterest in all Curzon's life; but he continued loyally to support the new Government, and after the General Election of 1924 he resumed the post of Lord Privy Seal. But early in 1925 he fell suddenly ill at Cambridge, and on 20th March he died in London, and after lying in state in Westminster Abbey was buried at Kedleston. He left no son and all his major titles expired. Lord Zetland wrote an admirable Life of him.

A distinguished traveller, writer and speaker, a good scholar and historian, a wit (his early lines "I'll sing you a lay" are well known), kind and genial though exacting, immensely meticulous in his work (he wrote most of his letters with his own hand), Curzon was one of the most remarkable Englishmen of his age. Of high birth, tradition and industry, he devoted himself to the public service and also to many other literary, artistic and patriotic interests, always in an informed, generous and magnificent manner. He did not attain the highest object of his ambitions— perhaps because of his dominating attitude—but no Viceroy of India ever earned or discharged that great office with a more honest eye to the prestige and benefit of India and of England. Fully conscious of his own undoubted talents and position, he was a splendid patriot and county magnate and generous to many public causes. Clemenceau's remark of him: *"orgeuil immense—justifié,"* was a not unfair tribute.

His rule in India ended an epoch. Even to-day, fifty years after he went there, people speak of "before" and "after" Curzon.

GILBERT JOHN ELLIOT
4TH EARL OF MINTO

25

EARL OF MINTO

1905-1910

GILBERT JOHN ELLIOT - MURRAY - KYNYN - MOUND, afterwards 4th Earl of Minto, was born in Wilton Crescent, London, on 1st July 1845, the eldest son of William Hugh, the 3rd Earl, by his cousin Emma, daughter of General Sir Thomas Hislop, who had commanded the Deccan army in the days of Lord Hastings' war against the Pindaris. His great-grandfather, the 1st Earl of Minto, had been Governor-General of India forty years previously. Under the latter's name the origin of his family has already been recorded.

First known as Viscount Melgund, he was educated at Eton and Trinity College, Cambridge, and at the age of nineteen joined the Scots Guards. As a young man he was a famous gentleman jockey, riding several times in the Grand National (the only Viceroy to do so) and winning the Grand Steeplechase of Paris in 1874. But he was no carpet soldier. He went out as war correspondent for the *Morning Post* with the Carlist army in Spain; and four years later he acted as Assistant Military Attaché to the Ottoman army in the Russo-Turkish War and saw much of the fighting. In 1879 he volunteered for the second Afghan War and served as A.D.C. to Sir Frederick Roberts, who two years later took him on to South Africa as his private secretary. In 1882 Rolly Melgund, as he was called, served with the Mounted Infantry in Egypt, where he was wounded, and for a short time he commanded the regiment.

In 1883 he married Mary, daughter of General the Hon. Charles Grey, a younger son of Lord Grey, the Prime

Minister. She was one of the best looking, most charming and popular girls of her day. For the next two years Melgund was Military Secretary to Lord Lansdowne when Governor-General of Canada, and in Riel's rebellion he acted as Chief of Staff to the Canadian forces and was present at the battle of Fish Creek.

After contesting a seat in Northern Ireland as a Liberal Unionist Melgund lived an active country life on his Roxburghshire estate until he succeeded his father in 1891. In his own county he was especially interested in the Volunteer movement; for he remained at heart a soldier.

Seven years later, at the age of fifty-three, he was appointed Governor-General of Canada, probably on Lord Lansdowne's recommendation. This office he held for nearly six years with exceptional success and universal approval. His simple straightforward manners and his reputation as a sportsman and a soldier endeared him to all, while his wife's kindness and beauty much enhanced his popularity. Both with Sir Wilfrid Laurier, the Canadian Premier, and Joseph Chamberlain, the Colonial Secretary at home, he worked on loyal and friendly terms. During these years the revenue and population of Canada increased by fifty per cent.—settlers poured in from England, the United States and Europe, the Klondyke Gold Mines were opened, Canadian forces took part in the South African War—their first military adventure overseas —and the long-standing Alaska Boundary dispute with the United States of America was settled. In 1902 the Duke and Duchess of York, later King George V and Queen Mary, spent five weeks in Canada—the first visit of a King and Queen of England—and in 1904 Minto left the Dominion. Seventeen years later, his eldest son was to marry a daughter of Canada.

Within twelve months of leaving Canada Minto was appointed Viceroy of India, where his success was hardly less than it had been in Canada; though when Lord Curzon heard who his successor was to be he is said to have asked, "Isn't that the gentleman who only jumps hedges?"

During Minto's term of office in India an agreement as to frontiers was made with Russia; and though much of his Indian policy was dictated by John Morley, the Secretary of State for India in Whitehall, for the domestic Indian reforms of 1909 Minto himself was mainly responsible. He added a native member to his Viceroy's Council in the face of much criticism and opposition, and he led the way to more liberal government. Even when an attempt was made on the lives of Lady Minto and himself at Allahabad he refused to desert his beliefs. His soldierly bearing and qualities appealed particularly to the Indian princes, who saw in him the type of an English gentleman and with whom his relations were exceptionally friendly; probably no Indian Viceroy was so universally liked and so widely respected: the loyalty and enthusiasm of the ruling Indian chiefs during the First World War was largely due to his shrewd and cheery camaraderie, while Lady Minto's constant interest and sympathy were also of the utmost help to him. The Indian Nurses' Association which she founded for Europeans in India, as she had previously started cottage hospitals in Canada, became and remains an unforgotten example of her work.

Minto left India in 1910 and on arriving home was given the Garter; but afterwards he took no part in political affairs, and in 1913 he fell ill, dying at Hawick on 1st March 1914. His eldest son is the present earl.

Minto, in the words of Lord Morley, was an able, active and conscientious soldier and public servant, "firm and always loyal and considerate to others, and sensible enough to understand the honesty of views with which he did not perhaps always agree, but often guiding and seconding by his popular personality the work of statesmen who laid down policy." His simple common sense and directness of mind and purpose, his sympathy and profound sincerity, did lasting good to the British name in India and eased the work of his successors in more difficult times.

From a photograph by Jeakins, Simla.

CHARLES HARDINGE

LORD HARDINGE OF PENSHURST

26

LORD HARDINGE OF PENSHURST

1910-1916

CHARLES HARDINGE, afterwards Lord Hardinge of Penshurst, was the second son of Charles Stewart, 2nd Viscount Hardinge, and grandson of the 1st Viscount, who had been Governor-General of India from 1844 to 1848. His father had been an M.P., an Under-Secretary of State and Chairman of the Trustees of the National Gallery. His mother, Lady Lavinia Bingham, daughter of the 3rd Earl of Lucan, died when he was six years old.

Born on 20th June 1858 at Highgate, he was educated at Harrow and at Trinity College, Cambridge, where he was a good oar and football player. He passed into the Diplomatic Service in 1880 and then served successively in Constantinople, Bucharest and Paris. His account of these years in *Old Diplomacy* makes fascinating reading, for it shews the early life of a man of character and intelligence who was determined to make good. In 1890 he married his first cousin, the Hon. Winifred Sturt, daughter of Henry, 1st Lord Alington, and niece of Lord Northbrook, who fifteen years earlier had been Viceroy of India.

Hardinge made a rapid and successful career in the Diplomatic Service, becoming Secretary of Legation at Teheran, Secretary of Embassy (Counsellor) at St Petersburg, Assistant Under-Secretary of State at the Foreign Office, and in 1904 British Ambassador at St Petersburg, when he was sworn a Privy Councillor. Two years later, while still under fifty, he was promoted to be Permanent Under-Secretary at the Foreign Office, one of the two most powerful and important positions in the Civil Service.

Well versed in his profession, popular in society, an ambitious, cultivated and able man, he had become a close friend of King Edward VII, during the latter part of whose reign he acted as Minister in attendance on the King during his various Continental journeys. The knowledge of foreign Courts and their leading figures which he thus acquired was of the greatest value; his wife was also attached to the Royal Household.

Hardinge was now at the very centre of affairs; his opinion and his conduct of business were highly regarded in the Cabinet, for he was known to be both an alert and a safe man. In 1910 he was chosen by Asquith and Morley to be Viceroy of India, a post that Lord Kitchener had long coveted; and he was then made a peer, though he said that he would have preferred to have waited until later for this honour. Three main features distinguished his term of office: (1) the Delhi Durbar held in 1911 to celebrate King George V's accession. This was a triumph of organisation and ceremony held in a vast and specially built camp and attended by all the Indian princes in their gorgeous paraphernalia (one proposed bringing two tigers with him). The management and layout of this pageant was largely due to Hardinge's personal supervision; it probably surpassed the greatest efforts of the Moguls and was one of the finest oriental displays that have ever been seen. (2) The declaration of the reunion of the two parts of Bengal which had been partitioned in Lord Curzon's time, a division which had led to much discontent and sedition. (3) The transfer of the capital of India from Calcutta to the more central situation of New Delhi. This annoyed the Calcutta merchants and British residents, but was otherwise an advantage now that contiguity to the sea was not a necessity.

In 1912, when Lord and Lady Hardinge were making their State entry into Delhi on an elephant, a bomb was thrown at them by which the Viceroy was badly wounded and for some weeks was laid up. The general result, however, was to evoke wide sympathy for him all over the country. But in July 1914 he lost his wife, who had gone home to England; and a few months later his elder son died of wounds received in France in the First World War.

During this war he successfully supervised the supply of Indian troops to Europe; and in the campaign in Mesopotamia it was on Hardinge that devolved the special duty of maintaining the transport and maintenance of troops and material to the expedition in the Persian Gulf. Though successful at first, this campaign did not go well later on, particularly as regards the medical arrangements and care of the sick and wounded. Hardinge went to Busra and up the Shat-el-Arab to see matters for himself; and some improvements were improvised. In the ensuing enquiry in London, though the responsibility was technically his, he was exonerated from blame, which was laid more directly on the Indian military authorities.

In the summer of that year the Prime Minister announced that because of his great services and in order to benefit by his experience Hardinge had been requested to remain on in India for another six months; and when he returned to England in the spring of 1916 he was made a Knight of the Garter.

As soon as he was back the Government again made use of his services. For the second time he was appointed Permanent Under-Secretary at the Foreign Office, in which capacity he later arranged for the Peace Conference in Paris. He also acted as Chairman of the Royal Commission on the Rebellion in Ireland. In 1920 he was appointed British Ambassador in Paris, the highest position in his profession, and here he remained until 1922, when he retired from the public service. He had led a long public life, he was becoming tired, and he did not get on with Curzon, the Foreign Secretary, who had also been his predecessor in India.

In later life he was concerned with business in the City. In 1923 and 1924 he acted as British Delegate for India in conferences at Geneva, and he attended the House of Lords regularly, though he seldom spoke; he used to sit on the Bishops' bench where a lay lord may not speak. He lived in London and at Penshurst, where his garden, his books and his Indian correspondents occupied him. There he died on 2nd August 1944 at the age of eighty-six. The present Lord Hardinge is his second and only surviving son.

Hardinge was one of the most distinguished public figures of his day. As a Civil Servant he had held two of the principal embassies and for ten years he had been the permanent head of the Foreign Office. He had staged the Delhi Durbar and the Paris Peace Conference, and during five crucial years he had been Viceroy of India and kept up a regular flow of native troops to the British Army. He had been the friend and adviser of King Edward VII, and he knew nearly every crowned head and leading statesman in Europe and many of those in Asia—he probably received more foreign orders of chivalry than any man living outside Royal circles. An accomplished linguist, a trained diplomat and an efficient administrator, his success had been due in the main to his own ability and diligence rather than to adventitious aids. A mine of information on conduct, people, places and past events, he was a kind, amusing and sympathetic friend. Yet he had his full share of personal sorrow; his wife, his elder son and his only daughter were all taken from him long before their time. But he did not relax in his work. Full of character, energy and determination, he left behind him the record of an active and brilliant man who had devoted himself to his own duties and to the interests of his country.

FREDERICK JOHN THESIGER
VISCOUNT CHELMSFORD

27

VISCOUNT CHELMSFORD

1916-1921

FREDERIC JOHN NAPIER THESIGER, afterwards 3rd Lord and 1st Viscount Chelmsford, was born at 7 Eaton Square, London, on 12th August 1868, the eldest son of Frederic Augustus, 2nd Lord, by Fanny, daughter of Major-General Heath, of the Bombay Army. His paternal grandfather, when Lord Chancellor in Lord Derby's Cabinet of 1858, had been raised to the peerage; and his father, a distinguished soldier who had seen much service in the Crimea, the Indian Mutiny and South Africa, had risen to the rank of General and had been Lieutenant-Governor of the Cape of Good Hope.

Thesiger was educated at Winchester and Magdalen College, Oxford, where he became a Fellow of All Souls, for he was a good classical scholar. After being called to the Bar he married in 1894 the Hon. Frances Charlotte Guest, daughter of the 1st Lord Wimborne, and he then served for some years as a member of the London School Board and of the London County Council. In 1905 he succeeded his father in the peerage and was successively appointed Governor of Queensland and of New South Wales, and in 1913 he was made a G.C.M.G.

In the First World War he went out to India as a Territorial captain with the Dorsetshire Regiment and the Royal Army Service Corps, being then nearly fifty years of age; and during these years he lost his eldest son from wounds received in Mesopotamia. While he was guarding the wireless station near Simla he was designated by Hardinge the Viceroy to take a mission of enquiry to the Persian Gulf on the medical mismanagement there; but before he had started he was suddenly appointed Viceroy as successor to Hardinge, who had been directed to offer him the post by Austen Chamberlain, the then Secretary of State. Chelmsford's brother-in-law, Wimborne, was Lord-Lieutenant of Ireland; his father had governed the Cape of Good Hope; and he himself had held similar posts in Australia. According to Hardinge, the names of four Tory peers had been submitted to Asquith, the Prime Minister, but "he would not look at them"; he preferred a Fellow of All Souls who was on the spot. It is said that Chelmsford had the letter in his pocket when his colonel told him that he ought to be doing something better than commanding a company.

During his five years of office Chelmsford was closely concerned in the so-called Montagu-Chelmsford plans for devolution which were inaugurated by Mr Edwin Montagu, who was first Under-Secretary and subsequently Secretary of State for India (1917-22). Montagu visited India himself and worked hard to persuade both the Viceroy and Indian opinion to accept his proposals. There had been considerable unrest and agitation for more self-government or Home Rule (Swaraj), led by Mr Gandhi; and various extensions of the native share in administration were made; the first Indian Governor of a Province, Lord Sinha in Behar, being appointed during Chelmsford's term of office.

During these years a wide influenza epidemic and famine spread all over the country and cost many lives; and when in 1919 riots of a revolutionary nature broke out at Amritsa, the religious capital of the Sikhs, some troops under Brigadier-General Dyer were employed in aid of the civil power. They fired on the mob; and a regrettable loss of life of nearly four hundred resulted, which was later the subject of a judicial enquiry and censure.

Early in 1921 the first meeting of the Indian Legislature and of the new Chamber of Princes was opened by the

Duke of Connaught; and in April of that year Chelmsford left India. On returning home he was made a viscount.

In the first Labour Government of 1924 he was for a short time First Lord of the Admiralty, and he subsequently acted for two years as Agent-General in London for New South Wales. In 1930 he was appointed Warden of Winchester, and in 1932 Warden of All Souls, his former colleges. In the following year he died suddenly at the age of sixty-four at Ardington House, Wantage, on 1st April 1933. The present viscount is his second son.

Chelmsford was a quiet and retiring man with a serious and lifelong devotion to municipal and public service. Like his father and his maternal grandfather, he had an interest in India and also much knowledge of colonial and local government, in which he played by no means a colourless but a respected and honoured part. Not a strong politician, he had progressive views to which he had the courage to adhere.

From a photograph by Lenare.

RUFUS ISAACS

MARQUESS OF READING

28

MARQUESS OF READING

1921-1926

RUFUS DANIEL ISAACS, afterwards Marquess of Reading, was born in London on 10th October 1860, the second son of Joseph Michael Isaacs, a fruit merchant of Finsbury Square, by Sarah, daughter of Daniel Davis. His family, of Jewish stock, was gifted with brains and initiative and was to supply a Lord Mayor to London in 1889. Slightly educated at University College School and in Brussels and Hanover, Rufus Isaacs took little interest in the family business and at the age of sixteen he went to sea as ship's boy, at a wage of ten shillings a month, on a Glasgow cargo boat where he defeated and knocked down the forecastle bully, for he was a boxer and ready with his hands. On this voyage he visited South America and India, where he was to be Viceroy half a century later.

On his return to England he again tried the family business, travelling occasionally to the Continent; but being still unattracted by it, in 1880 he became a clerk and later a member of the Stock Exchange. Having little capital or knowledge, he came to grief and was hammered, his debts remaining round his neck for many years. Disraeli had had a somewhat similar experience. Finally Isaacs turned to the Bar at the late age of twenty-four, for he had a fever of ambition, ability and energy. In 1887 he was called at the Middle Temple and in the same year he married Alice Edith, daughter of Albert Cohen, a Hamburg merchant.

His success at the Bar was almost phenomenal. He had a rapid, incisive and persuasive address, a finely modulated voice, an attractive appearance and manner, and he

worked amazingly hard. He spoke without notes and
never bullied witnesses. In his first year he made £500
and for the next twenty-five years he was engaged in a
number of famous actions and *causes célèbres* of the day,
among them Allen and Flood, Chetwynd *v.* Durham, the
Goudie, Hartopp, Taff Vale and Whitaker Wright cases.
When in 1904, just before the Liberals came into office,
he was elected M.P. for Reading, he was making £28,000
a year. The new Commercial court had opened a fresh
field of success for him; and his reputation kept pace with
his income.

In the House of Commons he soon made his mark,
becoming a friend of Lloyd George; and in 1910 Asquith
appointed him Solicitor-General, promoting him in a few
months to be Attorney-General. Two years later he was
sworn a Privy Councillor and given a seat in the Cabinet,
the first Attorney-General to sit there. In this capacity
he conducted several important Bills through the House.

During 1912 and 1913 he was much harassed by accusa-
tions connected with the purchase of shares in the Marconi
Company, of which his brother was managing director,
and in which he had foolishly bought some shares (though
only at the market price) in company with other Ministers;
but after a long and careful enquiry the House of Commons
exonerated him of any improper motive or action. In the
press of business he was often careless (and not very
successful) about his personal financial affairs. Despite
this trouble he was in October 1913 appointed Lord Chief
Justice of England in succession to Lord Alverstone.
He could always sleep at a moment's notice, and he used
to say that that fitted him to be a judge. A few months
later he was created a baron as Lord Reading.

On the outbreak of war in 1914 he was called into
counsel by the Cabinet and the Treasury, and he took
a large share in the financial legislation necessitated by
hostilities; indeed for many months he continued to work

day and night at this as well as at his judicial duties. As an acknowledgment of this double strain he was made a G.C.B. in June 1915. By that time Great Britain's balances in New York had disappeared and it was vital to get more credit. A Presidential election was in view; and the outlook was not favourable. It was accordingly determined to send an Anglo-French Loan Mission to the States; and Reading was chosen as its leader.

With his expert advisers he arrived in New York in September. He already had friendly connections with the great banking house of J. P. Morgan; and his tact, eloquence and statesmanship enabled him to carry through his mission. He negotiated with Ministers and bankers, addressed public and private meetings, and within a month had raised a loan of 500 million dollars. He then returned to his work in London, and in June 1916 was made a viscount.

Early in the following year the United States came into the war; and Reading was sent to Washington and Ottawa as High Commissioner to supervise and co-ordinate the immense orders for material which the British Government was placing in America.

On his return to London in November he was raised to an earldom, and two months later he was appointed Ambassador in Washington. Mr Page, then American Ambassador in London, writing to President Wilson, said of him: "He is one of the ablest Englishmen living, not so spectacular as old Dizzy, but far sounder. In a concrete job he will succeed better than any man." *The Times* called him the "Government's financial right hand." Two difficult problems with which he had to deal during his embassy were the temporary command of the fresh American troops by British generals and the sale to India of large consignments of silver to meet the shortage of currency there. In August 1918 he went back for consultation to London, having received honorary degrees at all the major American universities, a unique honour for a foreigner.

After the Armistice Reading paid a brief visit to Paris as a member of the Supreme Council, and he then returned to Washington to take leave on the completion of his mission in May 1919.

For some months he now resumed what seemed the comparatively dull routine of trying causes and travelling circuit, until early in 1921 he was appointed Viceroy of India in succession to Lord Chelmsford. He was now over sixty years of age and had behind him a quarter of a century of gruelling work; but his thirst for further and fresh activities had not diminished. The Greco-Turkish war had greatly exacerbated Moslem feeling in India; and the support given to the Greeks by the Government in London made the position delicate. Reading deprecated this policy and pressed for his advice to be made known, so Edwin Montagu, the Secretary of State for India, released the relevant despatch without asking the Cabinet's leave, and in consequence had to resign his office. Meanwhile in India Reading was exercising a wide and moderating influence on domestic policy, for he had a racial flair for the East. His Liberal principles were known, and his judicial attitude was appreciated.

In 1922 the Prince of Wales paid a visit to India; and in the following years there was much domestic legislation. The Press Acts were repealed; a protective tariff was inaugurated; the opium traffic was still further restricted; and the Indian marine was reorganised. The position of Indians in the Dominions and self-governing Colonies was also a constant subject of negotiation. In 1924 there were serious Hindu-Moslem riots at Kohat in the North-West Provinces, and these went on simmering for some time.

Early in 1925 Reading went home for three months, leaving Lord Lytton, Governor of Bengal, in charge. He returned to India in August, and was again faced with the continuing antagonism between Hindus and Moslems, as well as with the rapid rise of communal organisations which adversely affected the working of the provincial legislatures. During all his term of office Reading had maintained constant friendly relations with the ruling princes, as he also did with four successive Secretaries of State—tasks that were not always easy.

In April 1926 he finally returned to England and was immediately advanced, without consultation, to a marquessate, the first Englishman since Wellington to have risen in his lifetime to this rank from that of a commoner. His religion debarred him from the Garter. He was now for the first time in his life without occupation, and, having no pension, without very much income. So he turned again to the City, where his experience and mental endowments soon opened a new field for him. He joined the Board of Imperial Chemical Industries, of which he was later President; he became Chairman of United Newspapers, of the Palestine Electric Corporation and of Carreras Tobacco, and a director of the National Provincial Bank. Here his financial and legal knowledge, his high repute and position, were of the first importance; and he devoted himself to the interests of his companies with his usual industry and acumen.

He still kept up his connection with India and with the India Office, but he remained always opposed to the grant of Dominion status; the time, he thought, for that had not yet come. For the depressed classes and for those of his own faith in Europe he felt and shewed constant sympathy and help.

In 1928 he was appointed Captain of Deal Castle, and in that year he served his term as Treasurer of the Inner Temple, an office he had never yet found time to fill. In 1930 he led the Liberal delegation to the India Round Table Conference, where he occupied the key position.

In January of that year he had lost his wife, who had.long
been in poor health but had subordinated her interests to
his own. Her help and sympathy in England, America
and India had always been his constant stand-by.

On the formation of the National Government in the
summer of 1931 Reading became for a few months Foreign
Secretary and Leader of the House of Lords; but he took
no office on the reform of the administration in October.
The constant labour, day and night, and the journeys to
Paris and Geneva would have been too severe a tax on his
strength. In that summer he married Stella, daughter of
Charles Charnaud. She had been his late wife's private
secretary and has become well known for her many
beneficent activities in the leadership of Women's organisations. With her he went for a long holiday in Palestine
and Egypt to restore his health, and at Luxor he fell
dangerously ill with double pneumonia; but he made a
marvellous recovery.

After a visit to the United States for some ceremonies
he was appointed in 1934 Lord Warden of the Cinque
Ports, and thereafter he lived much at Walmer Castle,
where he was near to the sea which he so much loved. But
his strength had long been overtaxed; and after a short
illness he died full of honours at 32 Curzon Street, on
30th December 1935, at the age of seventy-five. The
present marquess is his only son.

Few people of our days have had a more remarkable,
rapid and romantic career with more successes in so many
different directions than Lord Reading. An abstemious
and healthy man, his handsome appearance, his clear
understanding and address, his diplomatic manner and
financial experience and his many popular social gifts
inspired those with whom he came in contact with a real
affection, and enabled him to fill some of the highest places
in the State with a general approval and admiration that
have rarely been surpassed.

Sir O. Birley pinx.

EDWARD WOOD

LORD IRWIN
EARL OF HALIFAX

29

LORD IRWIN, EARL OF HALIFAX

1926-1931

EDWARD FREDERICK LINDLEY WOOD, later Lord Irwin and Earl of Halifax, was born on 16th April 1881, at Powderham Castle, Devon, the fourth son of Charles, 2nd Viscount Halifax, by Lady Agnes Elizabeth Courtenay, only daughter of William, 11th Earl of Devon. The Woods had been established in the West Riding of Yorkshire since the early seventeenth century and were the owners of considerable agricultural and coal-mining estates. The 1st viscount, Sir Charles Wood, had been a distinguished Whig statesman, and after taking a double first at Oxford had sat in the House of Commons for forty years and been successively Chancellor of the Exchequer, President of the Board of Control, First Lord of the Admiralty, Secretary of State for India and Lord Privy Seal, until he was raised to the peerage in 1866. A man of wide repute and influence, with a thorough knowledge of Indian affairs which he had managed in London in the days of the East India Company and of the Crown, before and after the Mutiny, he lived to the age of eighty-four. His son, the 2nd viscount, who lived to the age of ninety-four, was a staunch and prominent High Churchman, an Ecclesiastical Commissioner and President of the English Church Union for forty years, a greatly respected figure in Yorkshire.

Edward Wood while still a boy became his father's heir by the death of his three elder brothers. He was educated at Eton and Christ Church, where, like his grandfather, he took first-class Honours, and was then elected a Fellow of All Souls. In 1909 he married Lady Dorothy

Onslow, daughter of William, 4th Earl of Onslow, and in the following year he became M.P. for Ripon. He was soon recognised as a promising and popular member of Parliament, for he had both character and courage, qualities which always appeal to the House of Commons. Like his grandfather, he already had the makings of a statesman; and like his father, he was a loyal and convinced Anglican; he was also a keen and practised rider in the hunting field and was Master of the Middleton Fox-hounds. In the First World War he served in France as a major in the Yorkshire Dragoons, his local Yeomanry regiment, being mentioned for his services in despatches.

In 1917 he was made Assistant Secretary at the Ministry of National Service, and four years later he was transferred as Under-Secretary to the Colonial Office. Here he did well, for he was serious, ready and courteous. In 1922 he was appointed President of the Board of Education and a Privy Councillor, entering the Cabinet at the age of forty; and in the following year he became Minister of Agriculture and Fisheries. He was also a personal friend of Arthur Balfour, Stanley Baldwin and Neville Chamberlain, who all had a high opinion of his merits, and he was regarded by many of the younger Conservative M.P.s as the future leader of their party.

At the end of 1925 Edward Wood was selected as Viceroy of India to succeed Lord Reading, and he was then raised to the peerage as Lord Irwin. He went out in April 1926; and his time in India coincided almost entirely with the active rise of Congress and the widespread and increasing agitation for Swaraj. The recent World War had encouraged this movement towards independence by shewing that the West was not invincible. Irwin's natural sympathies were not opposed to this desire; and his moderating influence was able to some extent to control and direct it. Its protagonist was the Mahatma Gandhi, an ascetic, enlightened and exalted Hindu politician who had become the apostle of the "British must go" policy, the keynote of which was to preserve Hinduism. But Gandhi and many of his followers were religious men, and they recognised and respected the genuine religious beliefs and conduct of the Viceroy. His tall, spare figure, thoughtful expression and quiet manners appealed to them; they admitted his *dignitas*, *gravitas* and *pietas*.

In 1928 a statutory Commission under Sir John (now Viscount) Simon visited India to examine the whole question of her relations with the Paramount Power. It was during their visit to India that Lord Irwin in October 1929 made his famous pronouncement which indicated the aim of the British Government: "that the natural issue of India's constitutional progress was the attainment of Dominion status." He had been in London for four months leaving Lord Goschen in charge. In this year, just before Christmas, when Lord and Lady Irwin were approaching New Delhi a bomb blew up a coach of the Viceregal train, though without hurting them.

The Report of the Simon Commission was not well received in India; and as Gandhi had started campaigning against the Salt Laws he had to be interned. After his release he had conversations with the Viceroy which led to the so-called "Delhi Pact," and he was subsequently a delegate to the Round Table Conference in London; but on his return to India he reverted to his policy of opposition. Meanwhile the Viceroy's critics accused him alternately of harshness and weakness.

All these years were full of great political difficulty; but a number of useful domestic laws and ordinances were passed in many states and provinces.

Lord Irwin returned to England in 1931 and was then made a Knight of the Garter. In the following year he was again appointed President of the Board of Education and in 1933 Chancellor of Oxford University in succession to Lord Curzon. Early in 1934 he succeeded his father as 3rd Viscount Halifax, and from then onwards he filled a number of the chief political posts. He did not seek office, office sought him. He was made Secretary of State for War and Lord Privy Seal in 1935; Lord President of the Council in 1937; and finally Foreign Secretary in 1938. In that capacity he had to deal with the imminence of hostilities with Germany. He visited Berlin and accompanied Neville Chamberlain to meet Mussolini in Rome and Hitler on the Rhine. Like Chamberlain (and Sir Robert Walpole), Lord Halifax was ready to go a long way to spare England another war. His efforts, however, were fruitless, and were afterwards stigmatised by some as "appeasement." During these years he was also a popular and successful leader of the House of Lords.

At the momentous change of Government in May 1940 he could almost certainly have had the offer of the Premiership had he so desired. But, like Curzon, he was a peer, and the voice of the country called for Mr. Churchill.

Three months later, on the death of Lord Lothian, Lord Halifax was appointed Ambassador to the United States, and there he remained for five years, travelling and speaking all over the country and maintaining the closest and most friendly relations with President Roosevelt in Washington. He also remained a member of the War Cabinet in London. Lord Halifax's tenure of his mission during the delicate and often crucial periods of the Second World War entitle him to be reckoned as a great Ambassador.

In 1944 he was raised to an earldom, and in 1946 on the termination of his embassy he was given the Order of Merit, the first ex-Viceroy to receive it. Two years later he was made Chancellor of the Order of the Garter. One of the few who can sway the House of Lords by a speech, he is now regarded as an elder statesman; he is a member of the House of Laity and of the Council of the B.B.C. and a D.C.L., or its equivalent, of twelve British, Canadian and American Universities.

Sir O. Birley pinx.

FREEMAN FREEMAN-THOMAS

MARQUESS OF WILLINGDON

30

MARQUESS OF WILLINGDON

1931-1936

FREEMAN THOMAS, afterwards Earl and Marquess of Willingdon, was born at Ratton in Sussex on 12th September 1866, the only son of Freeman Thomas of that place and of Yapton, by the Hon. Mabel Brand, daughter of Henry Bouverie, 1st Viscount Hampden, formerly Speaker of the House of Commons. His family, long settled in Sussex, was descended from Arthur Freeman, who had married a daughter of Sir George Thomas, Governor of the Leeward Islands in 1750; and their son Inigo, M.P. for Weobley, had taken the name of Thomas on inheriting his mother's property.

Freeman Thomas was educated at Eton and Trinity College, Cambridge, where he was a distinguished athlete, being Captain of the Cricket Eleven both at his school and university, thus wearing the coveted light blue cap for seven consecutive years. He was also a deft fives player, a good shot and a keen rider to hounds, being for some time Master of the Eastbourne pack.

In 1892 he married Marie Adelaide, daughter of Thomas, afterwards 1st Earl Brassey, a prominent Liberal, and the son of a wealthy contractor. He then took the surname of Freeman-Thomas. From 1897 to 1900 he served as A.D.C. to his father-in-law when Governor of Victoria; and on returning to England he was elected as Liberal M.P. for Hastings and later for Bodmin. He was good-looking, good-tempered, shrewd, a good mixer and very popular in the House of Commons; and when the Liberals came into office in 1905 he was appointed a Junior Lord of the Treasury and a Whip, a post for which he was eminently suited. Five years later he was promoted to the House of Lords as Lord Willingdon, being then appointed a Lord in Waiting.

In 1913 he was made Governor of Bombay, where his friendly and straightforward qualities in council and his abilities at outdoor sports at once made him an outstanding success. In the following year he lost his eldest son in the First World War. Five years later he was transferred as Governor to Madras, where he was as well liked as he had been in Bombay. In both presidencies he was much helped by his active and attractive wife, whom he called his "constant inspiration and encouragement," and he was generally considered, both in India and at home, as an ideal Governor. In 1924 he was the Delegate for India at the Geneva Conference; and on finishing his term at Madras he was advanced to a viscountcy. In 1926 Willingdon was sent as head of a mission to China to settle the terms of the Boxer Indemnity. He travelled by way of Canada, where his father-in-law had built the Grand Trunk Railway, and had then to traverse much of the Chinese Empire, moving between South and North to visit the rival War Lords and crossing their frontiers under heavy escorts. While he was in China he received the offer of the Governor-Generalship of Canada; and on his return to England he was made a G.C.M.G.

Willingdon was now a man of sixty, but very young for his age, a tried and experienced officer of the Crown. His work in the Dominion was facilitated by the new system under the Statute of Westminster of having a High Commissioner in Ottawa who was responsible for all official communications with the various departments in Whitehall, so that the Governor-General became only the constitutional representative of the Sovereign. This was followed by the exchange of diplomatic envoys between Canada and the United States and other countries.

In 1927 the Diamond Jubilee of the Canadian Federation

was celebrated by visits to Canada from the Prince of Wales and Stanley Baldwin, the British Prime Minister; the long-standing controversy between Canada and Newfoundland regarding the Labrador frontier was formally settled; and a new International Peace bridge was opened connecting Ontario with Buffalo in the United States. In 1929 Ramsay MacDonald also visited Canada.

The Willingdons had endeared themselves to the Canadians; he was called their most popular Governor-General; and on Lord Halifax completing his term of office in India there seemed to be no one more suitable for the place than one who had already served there for ten years and knew and was known to many of its leading figures. Four of Willingdon's predecessors in India, Elgin, Dufferin, Lansdowne and Minto, had all been Governors-General of Canada; but only once in the last century had a former Governor of a Presidency, Bentinck, risen to the highest place in India, though Lawrence had refused the Governorship of Bombay.

Willingdon, who was now given an earldom, took up his new office in 1931. He was the oldest Viceroy who had ever gone out to India, but he shewed few signs of age. He at once started travelling about the country by air, the first Viceroy to do so.

India was still mainly occupied with the Independence movement, though there was now an interval of comparative quiet; but in 1934 one of the greatest earthquakes ever known devastated many provinces and states and monopolised attention.

In 1935 self-government under responsible ministries was accorded by the British Parliament to eleven provinces of British India, their relations to the Central Executive being designed to some extent on a line with those of the Federal Constitution in the United States of America. During these years various measures were passed to regulate the Indian currency; and a commercial treaty was made with Japan—a rising competitor with India in trade and industry. All his duties Willingdon had carried out with exceptional success. He was immensely popular with the Rajahs, for his gallant bearing and open, friendly manner won the hearts of all. He fought against the divisions between English and Indian society. As Sir James Grigg says, "To any visitor he invariably conveyed the impression that his visitor was the one person on earth he most wanted to see."

In 1935 he had had some short leave in England, largely occupied with departmental work and formal entertainments. He said to the present writer: "My holiday will only begin when I step on board ship on my return journey." On his final return home in 1936 Willingdon was raised to a marquessate, and was later appointed Lord Warden of the Cinque Ports and Chancellor of the Order of St Michael and St George. His activity and devotion to duty remained undiminished; and in 1938 he led an important Good Will Mission, and in 1941 a Trade Delegation, to South America. Besides having been for twenty consecutive years a Governor or Governor-General in East or West, he had thus travelled in the service of the State from China to Peru.

His good health, good will and good nature gave him a happy life which he always enjoyed, working to the end. Full of honours, beloved by all who knew him, an honest and able patriot, he died in London on 12th August 1941, at the age of seventy-four. The present marquess is his younger and only surviving son.

From a photograph by Kinsey Bros., New Delhi.

VICTOR ALEXANDER JOHN HOPE

2ND MARQUESS OF LINLITHGOW

31

MARQUESS OF LINLITHGOW

1936-1943

VICTOR ALEXANDER JOHN HOPE, now Marquess of Linlithgow, was born on 24th September 1887, at Hopetoun House in that county, the eldest son of John Adrian Hope, 7th Earl of Hopetoun and later 1st Marquess of Linlithgow, by the Hon. Hersey Alice de Moleyns, daughter of the 4th Lord Ventry. The Hopes are an ancient Scottish family of large estates and of long public service. The 7th Earl had served as the first Governor-General of the Commonwealth of Australia from 1900 to 1902, when he had been raised a step in the peerage.

His son, the present marquess, first known as Lord Hopetoun, was educated at Eton. In 1908 he succeeded his father, and three years later he married Doreen Maud, daughter of Sir Frederick Milner, 7th Baronet. A good cricketer and golfer, he served throughout the First World War with the Lothians and Border Horse, on the staff, and in command of a battalion of the Royal Scots. From 1922 to 1924 he was Civil Lord of the Admiralty, and from 1924 to 1926 Deputy Chairman of the Conservative Party organisation. He was then appointed Chairman of the Royal Commission on Agriculture in India, with which he worked in that country from 1926 to 1928. On its conclusion he was made a G.C.I.E. and also a Knight of the Thistle. He then became Chairman of a Departmental Committee on Agricultural Distribution and Prices, of the Imperial College of Science and Technology, and President of the Navy League. In 1933 he was selected to be the Chairman of the very important Joint Parliamentary Select Committee on

K   145

Indian Constitutional Reforms. He thus acquired a wide first-hand knowledge, not only of the politics and administration, but also of general Indian affairs, and when in 1936 he was appointed Viceroy of India he probably knew more about the problems of that country than any of his predecessors had done, except perhaps Curzon.

His Viceroyalty of well over seven years was the longest there has been since India was transferred from the East India Company to the Crown in 1858. It fell in times of unprecedented difficulty, for during its earlier period the Viceroy had to face the task of putting into effect the Government of India Act of 1935, and from 1939 to 1943 he had the immense responsibility of organising India for war.

A tall, imposing man, who towered above the Indian rulers and his own bodyguard, Lord Linlithgow had both knowledge and judgment, and he managed his delicate task with an admirable degree of success. He was always ready to make the first move, and his published correspondence was marked by patience, sincere anxiety and appreciation of all the points of view put forward. His personal interest in the details of administration and his tireless industry compared with those of Dalhousie and Curzon. He was essentially a realist.

The early years of his Viceroyalty were marked by the first general election in 1937, under the Government of India Act of 1935, and by the introduction of the system of provincial autonomy it provided. At the elections the Congress Party obtained a majority in six of the eleven Provincial Assemblies. But they refused at first to take office, and it was only after explanations and reassurances by the Viceroy that they consented to do so. They remained in office until the outbreak of the war in 1939. But in October of that year the Congress Governments resigned; and the Governors had then to take over power. As arrangements to bring the Federal part of the scheme

into operation were not yet complete, further action on it
was temporarily postponed.

The period 1939 - 43 was marked by repeated endeavours by the Viceroy to meet Indian political aspirations and to secure a friendly relation between this country
and the chief political parties in India, and by the organisation of India for war.

In October 1939 a statement of the intentions of the
British Government proved insufficient to secure Congress
support; and in August 1940 a further statement by the
Viceroy accepted the principle that the future constitution of India should, after the war, be prepared by Indians
themselves; and it also gave assurances to minorities. In
July 1941 the Governor-General's Council was expanded
and given an Indian majority; and a representative
National Defence Council was established. In the spring
of 1942, Sir Stafford Cripps' Mission made extensive and
far-reaching constitutional proposals, but again without
success; and there followed in the autumn of that year Mr
Gandhi's "Quit India" resolution, and the serious internal
disorders that succeeded it. No solution of the constitutional problem had been reached, despite continued
efforts, when Lord Linlithgow's term ended.

But while his repeated endeavours had borne little fruit
in the political field, the Viceroy's efforts for the organisation of India for war were an outstanding success. A
Defence of India Committee, presided over by Admiral
of the Fleet Lord Chatfield, had visited India from 1938 to
1939; and from the beginning of the war, India's readiness
to help in men and munitions was made known. A force
of over two million men, containing material of first-class
fighting quality, was recruited for the Army; while India's
war potential in terms of industrial production and the
production of military weapons was also developed to the
highest degree; and in this the Viceroy took the closest
interest, and also in the equally important matter of

supply; indeed, India's vast war contribution in men, money and material was due in no small degree to his steady and consistent personal stimulus and support.

In 1943 Lord Linlithgow returned home after seven and a half years as Viceroy. He had borne an exceptionally heavy burden. Although he had not found the solution of the political problem, he had made clear the anxiety of the Government at home to meet India's national aspirations, while in the organisation of India for war he had provided the firm hand and cool judgment that were called for at a most critical time. He was one of the few who considered military danger to be as likely to come from the East as from the West. He wanted to build a road from India to Burma over the mountains, but the expense was prohibitive and the soldiers wanted other things more.

In much of his work Lady Linlithgow had been a constant help to him, and particularly by her establishment of a tuberculosis fund and campaign throughout India.

On his return Lord Linlithgow was made a Knight of the Garter, which he alone outside the Royal circle now holds in addition to the Thistle. In 1944 and 1945 he served as Lord High Commissioner to the Church of Scotland. He is Chancellor of Edinburgh University, Captain of the Royal Company of Archers, Lord-Lieutenant of Linlithgow and Chairman of the Midland Bank.

Simon Elwes pinx.

ARCHIBALD WAVELL

EARL WAVELL

32

EARL WAVELL

1943-1947

ARCHIBALD PERCIVAL WAVELL, now Earl Wavell, was born on 5th May 1883 at Colchester, the son of Major-General Archibald Graham Wavell by Lilian Mary, daughter of Richard Percival of Springfields near Bradwell in Cheshire. His family had a long history of public and military service. They had been sheriffs and members of Parliament, Cavaliers in the seventeenth century, and had given nine mayors to the city of Winchester. Both his grandfather and father had been general officers, the former serving in the Peninsular War and the latter in command of the Highland Brigade in South Africa, after which he settled near Cranborne Chase in Dorset.

Archibald Wavell took a scholarship at Winchester, where he was considered one of the best brains that famous school had sent to the Army. He passed fourth into Sandhurst and in 1901 was commissioned in the Black Watch—his father's regiment. After seeing some slight service in South Africa he was sent to India, where he devoted himself to the serious study of his profession, to learning languages and to travel and sport, much as Sir William Robertson had done twenty years earlier. At the age of twenty-five he passed first into the Staff College, and was sent to Russia to learn the language. Here again he travelled about the country, and was attached to the Russian Army on manœuvres. On his return home he was appointed first to the Military Training Department and later to the Intelligence Branch of the General Staff.

He was early in France in the First World War, serving as a brigade-major, and later as liaison officer in the

Caucasus and Egypt, where he was a friend of T. E. Lawrence. In 1915 he married Eugenie, daughter of Colonel Owen Quirk, C.B., The Welsh Regiment. At the age of thirty-three he was already a brevet lieutenant-colonel; and after a short spell on the staff of the High Command at Versailles he was again in Egypt under Lord Allenby, where he became a brigadier-general and Chief of Staff to an Army corps. Here again he much increased his knowledge of the Near and Middle East. At the end of the war, on the scaling down of ranks, he rejoined his regiment at Cologne as a major, but was soon appointed an A.A.G. at the War Office and went on regularly with the study of his profession.

By 1930, at the age of forty-seven, he was a brigade commander in England, specialising in training and physical fitness; and three years later he was promoted major-general. In 1937 he was appointed to command the troops in Palestine, and for a short time he held the Southern Command in England, being then knighted and created a K.C.B. In the following year he was made Commander-in-Chief, Middle East; and was soon plunged in a major rôle into the Second World War.

During 1940-41 he fought a series of largely simultaneous campaigns in the Sudan, Eritrea, Italian Somaliland, Abyssinia, Libya, Greece, Crete, Syria and Irak, of varying fortunes, and probably of a diversity, importance and extent unequalled in military history; policy was often imposed on strategy. In the winter of 1940 with about 80,000 troops he made a rapid advance against a far greater Italian force (415,000) along the North African coast into Tripolitania, a welcome and encouraging stroke for the Allies at a very low ebb of the war. General Fuller calls this one of the most audacious campaigns ever fought; "in two months, December 1940-February 1941, an army of ten divisions was destroyed." But Wavell was obliged to detach divisions to Greece and to the Sudan; the Germans arrived in force; and in March he had to retire on Egypt. There was the presage of more danger further East, and in the summer of 1941 he changed places with Sir C. Auchinleck and became Commander-in-Chief in India: while there he had also for a time the administrative control of the earlier part of the Burma campaign and of the South-West Pacific theatre of war. He was the first Allied general to command a combined force of British and American troops; there were few fully trained formations left in India.

In 1943 he was promoted Field-Marshal, and on the retirement of Lord Linlithgow he was appointed Viceroy of India, and created a viscount. His military responsibilities did not cease, for during this, as during the earlier World War, invaluable assistance was given to the British Forces by native troops from India, who suffered over a hundred thousand casualties. These had to be fed, as had India, now that Siam and Burma were no longer supply areas. During all the time of his Viceroyalty the long and complicated negotiations on the question of self-government continued between the Cabinet in London and the Indian Congress, but no agreement acceptable to both was arrived at, and tension remained high. The Muslims were not as well organised as the Hindus.

In March 1947, after the war was over, Lord Wavell resigned his office. It may be that he did not see eye to eye with the Home Government on the method and time-table by which the liquidation of British rule in India was to be completed. He was given an earldom; and was subsequently appointed to the historic post of Constable of the Tower of London.

He maintains his sporting and literary interests. He has had more than a dozen bones broken at different times, and is the author of several books on military subjects and an anthology of light verse.

Lords Cornwallis, Hastings, Hardinge and Wavell are

the only regular soldiers of high rank who have also been Governors-General of India. Three of them had previously been offered the Command-in-Chief in India; but only Lord Wavell held it.

Lord Wavell admits to a liking for "unorthodox soldiers, and a leaning to the unorthodox in war," though he ascribes to himself "a lack of enterprise in straying from the regular path of soldiering." His varied campaigns in three continents have probably given him more military experience than any commander now living. Like his predecessors, Lords Halifax and Linlithgow, he is a listener rather than a talker. One of his favourite remarks is supposed to be "I see."

Sir O. Birley pinx.

LOUIS MOUNTBATTEN

EARL MOUNTBATTEN

33

EARL MOUNTBATTEN

April to August 1947

LORD LOUIS MOUNTBATTEN, now Earl Mountbatten of Burma, was born at Frogmore House, Windsor, on 25th June 1900, the second son of Admiral of the Fleet Prince Louis of Battenberg, afterwards first Marquess of Milford Haven, by Princess Victoria, daughter of Louis IV, Grand Duke of Hesse, and Princess Alice of Great Britain. The Battenberg family descend morganatically from an earlier Grand Duke of Hesse, and were distinguished for their talents and looks. Prince Louis, an extremely able sailor, was First Sea Lord at the beginning of the First World War, and after it was raised to the peerage, when he changed his name to Mountbatten. One of his daughters married Prince Andrew of Greece and is mother of the Duke of Edinburgh, and the other is Crown Princess of Sweden.

His second son, Louis, was educated at Osborne, Dartmouth, and Christ's College, Cambridge; and after serving in H.M.S. *Lion* and *Queen Elizabeth*, Lord Beatty's flagships, and in submarines during the First World War, he became Lieutenant R.N. in 1919. Three years later he married the Hon. Edwina Ashley, elder daughter of Wilfrid, Lord Mount Temple, and granddaughter of Sir Ernest Cassel, the well-known financier and friend of King Edward VII. He was mechanically-minded and able with his hands, and as a specialist in wireless and signals he became a Senior Instructor in the Royal Navy Signal School in 1929 and Fleet Wireless Officer in the Mediterranean, and Commander R.N. in the following year. He was known as a serious and daring officer with new if unorthodox views, and was marked out for promotion.

153

After commanding H.M.S. *Daring* he served for a time in the Admiralty Naval Air Division: being promoted captain in 1937 at a very young age for that rank. In the early part of the Second World War he saw a great deal of fighting and shewed much dash and inventive skill. He commanded H.M.S. *Kelly*, which was sunk off Crete, and the 5th Destroyer Flotilla in 1939.

In 1941 he was made a D.S.O. and after being posted to H.M.S. *Illustrious*, the aircraft carrier, he turned to administration. In 1942 he was appointed Chief of Combined Operations to succeed Admiral of the Fleet Sir Roger (later Lord) Keyes, becoming a member for certain purposes of the Chiefs of Staff Committee. General Eisenhower speaks of him at this time as known in America for vigour, intelligence and courage. He was then given the rank of Acting Vice-Admiral and was also made an Honorary Lieutenant-General and Air Vice-Marshal. In this new capacity he was closely concerned with the Commandos and Cross Channel raids and their technical machinery. This was the start of the aggressive side of the war, and in it he made a name for himself.

In 1943, as the result of the Quebec Conference, he was appointed Supreme Allied Commander of the South-East Asia Command. He had his headquarters at first at New Delhi, later at Kandy in Ceylon, and then at Singapore. His forces were made up of all three services, sea, land and air, both British and American, spread over Burma, the Indian Ocean and the Malay Archipelago. He had to work with Generals MacArthur and Stilwell and also with the Chinese Army, and was thus largely concerned with the successful termination of the campaign in Burma, where he used constantly to visit his troops. The operational conduct of much of the war against Japan was also in his hands, and he was directly responsible to the Combined Chiefs of Staff Committee. After the end of the war he was for some months in virtual control of the whole of South-East Asia, and as a recognition of his services he was raised to the peerage as Viscount Mountbatten of Burma and was later made a Knight of the Garter.

On the retirement of Lord Wavell early in 1947 Lord Mountbatten, who was much in the public eye, was appointed Viceroy of India, the first sailor and the last Englishman to hold that post. He took with him an exceptionally strong staff, including Sir Hastings (now Lord) Ismay, who had started his military life in India and had been Secretary to the Cabinet and Chief of Staff to Mr Churchill; Sir Eric Miéville, who had been Secretary to the Indian Executive Council and Private Secretary to His Majesty the King; and Lord Wavell's Private Secretary, now Sir George Abel. Lord Mountbatten found himself confronted with the extremely difficult task of compressing and shortening the proposed time-table for the transfer of power; and under his direction the long negotiations between the British Cabinet and the Indian Congress were at last ended, a measure, though not all, of his objects being obtained, as two Dominions instead of one were eventually set up. The position of the princes, some of whom had acceded to the new governments, was not at first greatly altered.

On the final grant of self-government to India Lord Mountbatten in August 1947 handed over power to the two Dominions of India (Hindustan) and Pakistan. He was then raised to an earldom, and at the special request of the new Government he temporarily accepted the post of Governor-General of the Dominion of India until June 1948, when he was succeeded by Mr Rajagopalchari, a distinguished high-caste Hindu, Pundit Nehru remaining as Prime Minister.

He had latterly been assisted by the presence of a High Commissioner for the United Kingdom, which enabled him to devote himself exclusively to Indian interests; and his attitude in this connection was recognised and appreciated.

In the short time he was in India he accomplished the remarkable feat of touring all the provinces and most of the native states. Lady Mountbatten, who had already worked hard throughout the war in high positions with the Order of St John of Jerusalem, also played a prominent part throughout this period.

On resigning his position in India Lord Mountbatten, who had been a substantive Rear-Admiral since 1946, was appointed Flag Officer in command of the First Cruiser Squadron, thus returning to the service in which his heart was fixed. He has now been promoted Vice-Admiral.

Lord Mountbatten is a man of good physical strength and health, and can turn his mind in many directions. He is a first-class polo player and has written a book on polo which is considered a classic on the subject. His connection with the Royal family, his naval and military reputation, his charm and personality, and his diplomatic ability and drive have been remarkable assets in his success; and to his initiative and goodwill and to the popular support of Lady Mountbatten have been largely due the comparatively peaceful transfer of power in India and the present solution.

It is possible that he was not particularly anxious to take on an unenviable task and to become the final successor of Warren Hastings, Dalhousie, Canning and Curzon; but he adapted himself to the circumstances; and his determination to succeed, his urbanity, infectious enthusiasm and whole-souled devotion to the cause he had in hand have undoubtedly secured him the gratitude of India and of His Majesty's Government. His daring and inventive resource may well have prevented civil war and retained India within the Commonwealth.

CONCLUSION

A SUMMARY of comparative facts in the lives of the thirty-three Governors-General and Viceroys (including Clive, who was only Governor of Bengal) may be of interest. From 1774 their designation was Governor-General (first of Bengal and later of India). From Canning's time in 1858 the title of Viceroy was added (though not in the patent); and that became the name commonly used.

Six of them were Scots, six Irish and the remaining twenty-one English. Fourteen were educated at Eton, six at Harrow, two at Winchester, two at Westminster and one at Haileybury; fourteen at Oxford, of whom ten were at Christ Church; and four at Cambridge. Five or six of these might be called scholars of some distinction. Most were sportsmen, a quality of importance in the nineteenth century. Several were masters of hounds. Twenty-one inherited peerages, and fifteen were sons of distinguished men.

In party politics few of them were extremists; but they frequently held views similar to those of the Government which appointed them. During the Regency friendship with the Prince of Wales was occasionally an element in their choice. Two were closely connected with Pitt and two were brothers-in-law of Castlereagh. There was one case of father and son holding the office, one of grandfather and grandson, one of uncle and nephew, and one of great-grandfather and great-grandson. Three were sons, and one was a brother of a Prime Minister.

Before their appointment to the Governor-Generalship six had been soldiers, five diplomats, three trained governors, one a sailor and one a lawyer; only four had been in the Indian Civil Service, though ten had previously served in India in some capacity: the rest had been working politicians. About a dozen could be called aristocrats—educated men of position and connection whose families had lived on their own lands for some generations; but very few were rich; nearly all were serious, able and diligent men.

All but one were married, but only nineteen have now living issue in the direct male line, and in the last forty-five years war has decimated their descendants. Lytton, Dufferin, Lansdowne, Minto, Hardinge, Chelmsford and Willingdon lost between them twelve sons and grandsons.

Nearly all the Viceroys went into public life young; though to none could Stendhal's aphorism apply, "*Quel malheur d'être ministre jeune.*"

Their average age for becoming Governor-General was forty-nine; though one, Dalhousie, was only thirty-five on his appointment, while Reading was in his sixty-first and Willingdon in his sixty-fifth year when he assumed office. Warren Hastings, Teignmouth, Wellesley, Amherst, Ellenborough, Ripon and Hardinge all lived to be over eighty.

Their average tenure of the Governor-Generalship was five and a half years; Warren Hastings held it for eleven, and the elder Elgin and Lord Mountbatten for under two years; Cornwallis was twice appointed to the post, as was Curzon (nominally). Their average length of life was sixty-nine; three died in office.

Two Presidents of the Board of Control, but no Secretary of State for India, became Governor-General or Viceroy; and as a rule that office was the last major episode in their careers. About half were notable apart from their work in India.

During the interim between the departure from India of a Governor-General and the arrival of his successor—in the early days sometimes several months—or on the rare occasions on which he was given leave of absence, the senior Member of Council or senior Governor of a Presidency filled his place.

Twenty were made peers or were promoted in the peerage. Of the rest, Warren Hastings and Lord William Bentinck, Lords Ripon, Lansdowne and Linlithgow, who were already marquesses, and the two Lords Minto and Elgin received no accession of rank, some at their own wish. The Viceroys were always made Privy Councillors and Grand Masters of the Star of India and the Indian Empire after the establishment of those orders; but only sixteen received the higher honours of the Garter, Thistle or St Patrick.

The Viceroy was always styled Excellency, as were the Governors of Presidencies—a title which was later extended to the Lieutenant-Governors of provinces.

The Viceroy's ceremonial dress was that of a first-class Civil Servant or of the Grand Master of the Star of India; but his normal official attire was usually a tall hat and frock-coat, his civilian status being thus emphasised.

As regards emoluments, these averaged about £20,000 a year, out of which it was seldom possible to save much; for though there were also considerable allowances the entertainment expenses were heavy, except when on tour and living in camps. Their initial outfit was also costly. The purchase from his predecessor of horses and carriages alone, a wasting asset, often cost a Viceroy several thousand pounds, paid from his own pocket. In the very early days, under the Company's rule, a Governor-General was no doubt able to make considerable financial gains; Clive and Warren Hastings certainly did, and even in the 1890's Lansdowne saved £20,000 in five years. In a few cases of hardship some compensation was paid on retirement by the Company; but for the last ninety years no pension has been given to a retiring Viceroy, though he has occasionally been made Lord Warden of the Cinque Ports or Constable of the Tower of London, both of which are in effect unpaid posts.

The Governor-Generalship of India has always been regarded as a high recognition of past or presage of future merit and rarely as a political reward. Usually offered to the best man available, it was seldom refused; George Canning, the 5th Earl Spencer, Lord Milner and F.-M. Sir Henry Norman are believed to have declined it. It was a post of such consideration that in the British Empire and in public esteem it ranked second only to that of Prime Minister. But it had its disadvantages. For an active politician or a large landowner to be absent for five years from Parliament and his estates and out of touch with domestic questions of the day at home might often be a handicap in later life; and latterly it became usual for an ex-Viceroy to abstain from party politics and to sit on the cross benches in the House of Lords for at least a year after his return from India, perhaps in order to discard some of his autocracy which Sir Herbert Edwards used to say combined the irresponsibility of the Great Mogul with the infallibility of the Pope. Lord Dufferin once remarked that twenty-five minutes in Pall Mall would take the conceit out of any Viceroy.

The Viceroy, whom Lord Curzon had called "Only a transient phantom in India," was probably the hardest-worked man in the whole country, for his work was arduous and incessant. Hedged in by lancers, chuprassies, mace-bearers, aides-de-camp and private secretaries (his principal private secretary, P. S. V., was sometimes a very great power in the land), and surrounded by a rampart of Civil Servants, he seldom spoke the vernacular; though latterly ceremonial was somewhat reduced and he had more contact with Indian society. Papers, files, boxes, interviews and conferences filled the mornings; ceremonies, inspections and visits the afternoons; and constant entertainments of one sort or another the evenings, which were often lengthened by more work far into the night. To many the social side was perhaps the most onerous; though here their wives played an invaluable part and also as the heads of many beneficent works for Indian women. But for family or private life there was little time; nor could domestic economy easily be regulated. The Viceroys had also to make long progresses up and down the country, sometimes extending to many weeks, and paid sporting visits to maharajahs who provided tigers or lesser game to shoot.

Their official residence was at first Fort William, and then Government House, Calcutta, a palace built by Wyatt in 1799 for Lord Wellesley, as has already been stated. It was replaced from 1912 by another palace built by Sir Edwin Lutyens at New Delhi. In the hot and longer season of the year they migrated to the Viceregal Lodge at Simla in the Lower Himalayas, a cool, charming and quiet home where more work could be done than in the heat of the plains. They also had a smaller country house at Barrackpur, near Calcutta, for week-end visits.

Character, courage and a good record were probably the chief factors in their selection. The better known, though not necessarily the most distinguished, were those who ruled in the eighteenth and early nineteenth centuries, when much was happening in the way of expansion and when the Governor-General was almost independent, being further removed in communication from the Cabinet at home than he was after the advent of the electric telegraph. But the hand of Whitehall often lay heavily upon him. The present writer remembers a Secretary of State for India telling him fifty years ago that, despite his Council, he had far more personal power at the India Office than he ever had at the War Office; while another used to say that he was always having to make up the Viceroy's mind for him.

Most of the Viceroys were active and industrious men from their youth up. The Scots were perhaps more distinguished for their application and tenacity, the Irish for their lighter hands and strokes of genius. In estimating their relative merits Lord Curzon placed Warren Hastings and Dalhousie first, and then Wellesley, Bentinck and Canning; and he recalled that for a quarter of a century, from 1884 to 1910, seven successive Viceroys were Etonians.

None of the long line failed in integrity, and few in ability. According to the standards of their times they can compare advantageously with the great proconsuls of the Roman, Russian or Chinese Empires. In the words of Prince Bismarck, a not unfriendly critic, "Were the British Empire to disappear, its work in India would remain one of its most lasting monuments." For ninety years, except for border engagements, no battle was fought on Indian soil; and it is worthy of remark that during a period of 173 years, from 1774, when Warren Hastings took office, until 1947, when Lord Mountbatten resigned it, out of thirty-two British Governor-Generals, autocrats appointed arbitrarily from the other side of the world to rule an alien and largely illiterate population, only one has been assassinated; while in exactly the same space of time and from exactly the same number of Presidents of the United States of America, freely elected by their own civilised compatriots, three have fallen by that fate. The "Lord Sahib" was regarded by rajah and ryot alike as the Father of his people; he filled a station as exalted as that of a king and as powerful as that of a dictator: to a quarter of the world's population he was a remote and venerated god. Yet it may safely be claimed that the British rulers of India have never failed to protect and promote the interests and well-being of the many hundreds of millions committed to their charge, and by so doing to enhance their own prestige and that of the country which gave them birth.

LIST OF GOVERNORS-GENERAL AND VICEROYS OF INDIA

Governors of Bengal

1758-1760 and 1765-1767 Lord Clive.
1772-1774 Warren Hastings.

Governors-General

1774-1785 Warren Hastings.
1786-1793 Marquess Cornwallis.
1793-1798 Sir John Shore, Lord Teignmouth.
1798-1805 Earl of Mornington, Marquess Wellesley.
1805 (2nd time) Marquess Cornwallis.
1807-1813 Earl of Minto.
1814-1823 Earl of Moira, Marquess of Hastings.
1823-1828 Earl Amherst.
1828-1835 Lord William Bentinck.
1835-1842 Earl of Auckland.
1842-1844 Earl of Ellenborough.
1844-1848 Viscount Hardinge.
1848-1856 Marquess of Dalhousie.
1856-1858 Earl Canning.

Governors-General and Viceroys

1858-1862 Earl Canning.
1862-1863 Earl of Elgin.
1863-1869 Lord Lawrence.
1869-1872 Earl of Mayo.
1872-1876 Earl of Northbrook.
1876-1880 Earl of Lytton.
1880-1884 Marquess of Ripon.
1884-1888 Marquess of Dufferin.
1888-1894 Marquess of Lansdowne.
1894-1899 Earl of Elgin.
1899-1905 Marquess Curzon.
1905-1910 Earl of Minto.

LIST OF GOVERNORS-GENERAL AND VICEROYS

1910-1916 Lord Hardinge of Penshurst.

1916-1921 Viscount Chelmsford.

1921-1926 Marquess of Reading.

1926-1931 Lord Irwin, Earl of Halifax.

1931-1936 Marquess of Willingdon.

1936-1943 Marquess of Linlithgow.

1943-1947 Earl Wavell.

1947 (April to August) Earl Mountbatten.

SENIOR MEMBERS OF COUNCIL OR GOVERNORS OF PRESIDENCIES
WHO ACTED AS GOVERNORS-GENERAL DURING INTERIM PERIODS

During the occasional interim periods between Viceroys or when they were on leave the Government was administered by the Senior Governor of a Presidency or a senior Member of Council.

1785-1786	Sir John Macpherson.
1798	Sir Alured Clarke.
1805-1807	Sir George Barlow.
1823	John Adam.
1828	W. B. Bayley.
1835	Sir Charles (afterwards Lord) Metcalfe.
1863	Sir Robert (afterwards Lord) Napier of Magdala.
1863	Sir William Denison.
1872	Sir John Strachey.
1872	Lord Napier of Merchistoun.
1904	Lord Ampthill.
1925-1926	Earl of Lytton.
1929	Viscount Goschen.
1934-1936	Hon. Sir George Stanley.

SOME LEADING EVENTS IN INDIAN HISTORY

1526	Baber, a Mongol princeling from Central Asia, invades the Punjab.
1556	Akbar, his grandson, founds the Mogul Empire.
1600	Queen Elizabeth grants a Charter to the East India Company.
1639	Fort St George (Madras) built.
1661	Bombay ceded to England by Portugal.
1688	Calcutta (site) bought by the English.
1658-1707	Aurungzib, great-grandson of Akbar. Zenith of Mogul Empire, which declines; and Southern India becomes independent.
1743	War between French and English settlements.
1751	The Afghans take the Punjab.
1751	Clive takes Arcot.
1756	Massacre of English in Black Hole of Calcutta.
1757	Clive retakes Calcutta and wins battle of Plassey.
1765	Bengal, Behar and Orissa revenues granted to English.
1768	Carnatic ceded to English.
1773	Supreme Court established at Calcutta by Warren Hastings.
1775	Benares ceded to English.
1779	First Mahratta War.
1784	Board of Control set up by Pitt.
1788	Warren Hastings impeached.
1791-1793	Cornwallis takes Bangalore; and settles revenue in Bengal.
1795	Warren Hastings acquitted.
1799	Seringapatam taken.
1803	Second Mahratta War; Sir A. Wellesley wins battle of Assaye; the Mogul Emperor becomes a British pensioner.
1817	Pindari War.
1824	1st Burmese War.
1829	Suttee (widow burning) declared illegal.
1833	China trade monopoly abandoned.
1835	Thugs suppressed.

1838	1st Afghan War.
1842	Retreat from Kabul; Kabul reoccupied.
1843	Sir Charles Napier wins battle of Miani and annexes Sind.
1846	1st Sikh War. Gough wins battle of Sobraon.
1849	2nd Sikh War; Capture of Mooltan by British; Indecisive action at Chillianwalla; Gough wins battle of Gujerat; Punjab annexed.
1852	2nd Burmese War; Pegu annexed.
1856	Oudh annexed.
1850-1856	Railways, telegraphs, cheap postage, Ganges Canal and three universities at Calcutta, Madras and Bombay opened in these years by Dalhousie.
1857	Indian Mutiny (sieges of Delhi, Lucknow, Cawnpore, Gwalior).
1858	Government of India transferred to the Crown; Governor-General becomes also Viceroy.
1877	Queen Victoria proclaimed Empress of India at Delhi.
1878	2nd Afghan War.
1879	Sir F. Roberts takes Kabul.
1880	British defeat at Maiwand; Roberts relieves Kandahar.
1886	3rd Burmese War; Annexation of Upper Burma.
1892	Indian Councils Act.
1909	Morley-Minto Reforms.
1911	Delhi Durbar; Bengal made a Presidency.
1912	Capital transferred to New Delhi.
1914-1918	Indian troops take part in First World War.
1917	His Majesty's Government's announcement (Mr Montagu) that their policy was "the increasing association of Indians in every branch of administration and the gradual development of self-governing institutions, with a view to the progressive realisation of responsible government in India as an integral part of the British Empire." Followed by— The Montagu-Chelmsford Report and—
1919	The Government of India Bill, implementing the Montagu-Chelmsford proposals.

1921	Indian Legislature and Chamber of Princes inaugurated.
1923	Burma made a Governor's province.
1928-1929	Lord Simon's Commission visits India.
1929	Lord Halifax's statement regarding Dominion status.
1931-1932	India and Burma Round Table Conferences.
1933	Joint Select Committee of both Houses on Constitutional Reform.
1935	Government of India Act, and Government of Burma Act.
1936-1937	First elections for new Indian Provincial Legislatures.
1937	Burma separated from India; Provincial autonomy comes into operation in India.
1939-1945	Second World War, in which Indian troops again take part.
1940	Moslem League Resolution adopting the Pakistan policy.
1941	Burma overrun by Japanese.
1942	Sir Stafford Cripps' Mission to India.
1944	Liberation of Burma from Japanese.
1946	Cabinet Mission to India.
1947	Passing of Indian Independence Act; Two Dominions of India and Pakistan created. 15th August.
January 1948	Burma leaves Commonwealth.

INDEX

[The surnames of peers are omitted when identical with their titles.]

Abdurrahman Khan, 95, 98, 103, 114

Abercorn, James Hamilton, 1st Duke of, 105

Abel, Sir G., 155

Aberdeen, G. Gordon, 4th Earl of, 72

Aberdeen, John Campbell Gordon, 1st Marquess of, 111

Abyssinia, 150

Acheson, Lady Mary, 51, 54

Addington, Henry, 37

Adige, battle of, 51

Agra, 33, 79

Ajmir, 87

Akbar, 1

Akbar Khan, 56

Alaska, 120

Albuera, battle of, 64

Alexander of Macedon, 1

Alington, H. G. Sturt, 1st Lord, 89, 123

Allahabad, 12, 73, 121

Allenby, E. H. H., 1st Viscount, 150

Alost, 42

Alverstone, R. Webster, Viscount, 132

Amherst, F. M., Lord, 47

Amherst, W. P., Earl, 47-49, 52, 158

Amherst, Lieut.-General W., 47

Ampthill, A. O. V. Russell, 2nd Lord, 116

Amritsar, 128

Amyand, Anna Maria, 37

Amyand, Sir George, 37

Andaman Islands, 87

Antwerp, 42

Arabi Pasha, 102

Archer, Thomas, Lord, 47

Archer, Hon. Sarah, 47, 49

Arcot, 9

Ardagh, Sir J., 106

Ashley, Hon. Edwina (Lady Mountbatten), 153, 156

Asquith, H. H., Earl of Oxford, 99, 108, 111, 124, 128

Assaye, battle of, 166

Athens, 77

Auchinleck, Sir C., 151

Auckland, George Eden, 2nd Lord and 1st Earl of, 55-58, 60

Auckland, William Eden, 1st Lord, 55

Augustus, 3

Aurungzib, 1

Australia, 145

Ava, King of, 2, 48

Ava, Archibald Blackwood, Earl of, 104

Ava, 2, 104

Baber, 1

Badajos, battle of, 63

Bahadur Shah, 73

Baldwin, Stanley, Earl, 138, 143

Balfour, A. J., Earl of, 105, 116, 138

Bangalore, 23

Baring, Evelyn, Earl of Cromer, 89, 91

Baring, Thomas, 90

Barlow, Sir George, 34, 38

Baroda, Gaekwar of, 90

Barrackpur, 49, 161